Britain's Spiritual Inheritance

Our revival history, our prophetic heritage

DIANA CHAPMAN

RIVER
PUBLISHING

River Publishing & Media Ltd
Barham Court
Teston
Maidstone
Kent
ME18 5BZ
United Kingdom

info@river-publishing.co.uk

ISBN 978-1-908393-23-4
Printed in the United Kingdom

Contents

What Others Are Saying...

One of the saddest verses in Scripture is found in Judges 2: 10: *'another generation grew up who knew neither the Lord nor what he had done for Israel.'* The stories of God's miraculous intervention were no longer being told and as a consequence God's people began to lose their way. Diana Chapman reminds us of what God has done in our land. And when we are reminded, hope rises that God can do it again in our time. Read and be inspired.

Billy Kennedy
Leader, Pioneer Network; Team Leader, New Community, Southampton

For the last few years I have followed the trail of past revivals both in the UK and USA. This has led me to trace the footsteps of the Wesleys, George Whitfield, Jonathan Edwards and others. I have visited Epworth in rural Lincolnshire, Northampton Massachusetts, Princeton University and old Moravian burial sites. I therefore read Diana's book, which is immersed in the richness of past revivals, with great interest. I have found it of great value to re-dig some of those ancient wells and along with many others long to see God moving powerfully in His world. Highly recommended!

Stuart Bell
Senior Leader, New Life Lincoln; Leader, Ground Level Network.

Diana has caught hold of the treasure of our national Christian heritage. We have people and places pulsating with history that tell of the glory of God which has been deposited on these Islands. Revivalists: get excited about this book!

Stewart Keiller
Leader of Bath City Church

If you have a heart for the UK and loved reading *God's Generals* then this book is a must for you! A wonderful overview of revival history in Britain that encourages us to keep running our own race.

Hugh and Ginny Cryer
Culture Changers

Foreword

Britain's Spiritual Inheritance is an important book—a very important book. Author Diana Chapman has successfully captured the burning embers of past moves of God and embedded them into these pages.

Be prepared to burn in your heart. I can't imagine any other outcome. As she walks us through the rich history of Britain's revivals and revivalists, we are more and more touched and inspired by what God made available to those who gave everything to see the Kingdom come.

Books like this are vital. Not only do they reveal our history with God; they create a prophetic momentum for what is about to happen. Testimonies always prophesy to those who are hungry for more.

The lack of revival and/or awakening is never on God's end of the equation. He is always willing and ready. While I expect *Britain's Spiritual Inheritance* to have great impact on the UK, I'm hoping its potency will be released to the nations of the world.

Bill Johnson, Senior Pastor of Bethel Church, Redding, CA
Author of *When Heaven Invades Earth* and *Hosting the Presence*

Introduction

Every year, visitors from all over the world flock to Britain because of its history. Keeping the past alive is something we British do well.

I live within the shadow of Windsor Castle, the Queen's favourite Royal residence where thousands of tourists come each year. What most of them don't know is that on a wall at the base of the hill on which the castle stands is a small blue plaque.

It commemorates the site where three men, Robert Testwood, Henry Filmer and Anthony Pierson were burned at the stake in 1544 because of their stand for religious freedom. As they passed through the streets to their place of execution, they challenged the onlookers to hold fast to the truth of the gospel. Eye-witness accounts tell how the crowds were deeply moved by their bravery and cheerfulness.

This country has a history with God. The 'little' stories of men and women like the Windsor martyrs are given meaning because they become woven inextricably in the 'big' story of redemption. Likewise our lives are lifted from the ordinary as we partner with the Holy Spirit and become part of his-tory.

After all, we are all part of the same plot and it's important to understand what's gone on before our entrance, more important than you think.

Our history is full of people like Evan Roberts who 'prayed heaven down,' resulting in the Welsh Revival of 1904-05 when more than 100,000 people became Christians. Our land is full of places such as the Scottish Hebridean Islands, where between 1949 and 1952 the atmosphere was so charged with the presence of God that men fell on their knees by the roadside as they walked to work.

Great men of God such as John Wesley and Smith Wigglesworth had ministries marked by the miraculous. There is story after story, place after place where the Holy Spirit has moved powerfully and whole communities have felt the impact. Worldwide moves of God can be traced back to geographic locations and specific individuals.

This is our heritage. There is a spiritual inheritance that belongs to us, innumerable blessings that are ours, mantles to be worn once more. Revivals are in the bedrock of Britain. These places of past spiritual blessing, metaphorically called 'wells,' are all over this nation waiting to be unblocked. When this happens, the pure water which originated in heaven will be released once more. As in the days of Noah, let the fountains of the deep meet the floodgates of heaven and cause a flood (Genesis 7:1). Marx believed that by stealing a nation's history you could steal that nation. It's time to claim back what the enemy has stolen. Join me on a journey of discovery as I tell some of the stories in the first eight chapters, and then explore what it means to re-dig the wells and understand our spiritual inheritance in the remaining three.

I pray that the reader will be gripped by the way history can impact the present when it is given a biblical and prophetic perspective. Please continue reading, even if you hated history at school. Believe me, you will be hooked! This is the book I was born to write.

Awaken Britain

You're calling your beloved back to you
In these times we awaken to your truth
We're drawing near to you
We're drawing near to you

You're calling your bride back to you
To be pure and holy
We're drawing near to you
We're drawing near to you

Chorus

These wells of my heart are overflowing
These wells of my heart are overflowing
And your love, your love is never failing
And your love, your love is never failing

Your love unfailing, grace abounding
I surrender all to you

This song was written by Matt Bella while a student at the Bethel School of Supernatural Ministry in Redding, California. He visited Britain with a group from this school in March 2011 and blessed us as he released this song over our nation. (used with permission)

1
What Do These Stones Mean?

I will utter hidden things, things from old – what we have heard and known, what our fathers have told us. We will not hide them from our children; we will tell the next generation.

Psalm 78:2-4

All over Britain are chapels and church buildings: monuments to what God has done, how his Spirit swept into history. They were often birthed in revivals when men and women who had encountered heavenly glory earthed the fire. Behind each is a story waiting to be told, a mantle to be taken, a truth to be rediscovered, a well to be unblocked.

Yonder country is ours

In 1877 a young woman called Annie moved from London to a small village in the county of Berkshire on the banks of the River Thames to marry a gentleman farmer, Charles Tough. A devout Primitive Methodist, she was, in her own words, 'impressed by the godlessness of the young people.' On her first Sunday in the village, she set out armed with bundles of tracts and talked to 'big lads and girls who were romping on the common' about Jesus. (1)

The 'Prims,' as they were known, had emerged 20 years after the death of John Wesley to radicalise the Methodists who were becoming respectable and had lost some of the early fire.

Annie's fervour met with opposition but she resolved she would not rest until a chapel was built. Nine years later, after raising the money required, she achieved her goal and gathered men and women round her who built up the congregation. Many were won to the Lord, impacting the village community right up to the late 20th century.

Some years previously, two men, Thomas Russell and John Ride, had fallen on their knees on a snowy Ashdown Common in the same county and cried out, 'Lord, give us Berkshire'. After five hours of fervent prayer, Russell jumped up and declared as he pointed to the horizon, 'Yonder country is ours and we will take it!' (2) A revival followed and many Primitive Methodist congregations were established, especially in Berkshire where there were more nonconformist churches than in any other county.

On the street where you live

If we fast forward to 2012, the 'Prims' have been absorbed back in the Methodist denomination from whence they came. Annie Tough's chapel has a dwindling, elderly congregation, who for self-preservation made a plea in the local *Village News* with a poignant article entitled, 'Wanted – A Congregation.' It lamented their decline and predicted an imminent death unless people joined them.

I know this because this chapel is in the street where I live. All credit to this faithful remnant who want the testimony to be kept alive, but it's not numbers that they need – it's the original fire.

Many churches, like that Primitive Methodist Chapel, are either on the verge of closure or have already shut their doors, becoming bijou residences or warehouses or functioning as mosques or temples.

The average man or woman may be concerned about their value to the national heritage, but has no knowledge or interest in the rich spiritual history of such places and what they represent. Of course many historic denominations are thriving, having allowed winds of renewal to blow the cobwebs away and bring new life. Yet I wonder how many Christians truly understand the amazing spiritual inheritance that is theirs.

Do you know the story behind that old grey stone building with the unfriendly facade in your neighbourhood? It may contain hidden treasure and be a key to unlocking your community as you discover how it was birthed and the vision of the founding father or mother.

Our land shouts its own story for those who have ears to hear.

Like memorial stones in Israel

These old churches and chapels are like the memorial stones erected by the Israelites in the land of Canaan. When they had crossed over the Jordan on dry land at Gilgal, the Lord told Joshua that a man from every tribe was to take a stone from the middle of the river bed and pile them up as a memorial.

Why were they to do this? In the future when their children saw these stones and asked the question, 'What do these stones mean?' their fathers would say, 'That's where the Jordan parted...that's where the whole nation crossed on dry land' (Joshua 4:6-7, 22).

It would be an occasion to tell the story, to keep the testimony alive and remind future generations of the intervention of God into human history. During the course of the conquest of Canaan, seven memorials of stone were built to show where important victories took place or where the covenant was renewed. These memorial stones functioned as altars, sacred places where heaven and earth met.

Don't settle down

After the conquest of Canaan, Israel took possession of the land and each tribe settled in its inheritance. The Lord had given them everything they needed for a good life but he warned them:

When the Lord your God brings you into the land he swore to your fathers, to Abraham, Isaac and Jacob, to give you – a land with large, flourishing cities you did not build, houses filled with all kinds of good things you did not provide, wells you did not dig, and vineyards and olive groves you did not plant – then when you eat and are satisfied, be careful that you do not forget the Lord who brought you out of Egypt, out of the land of slavery. (Deuteronomy 6:10-12)

It seems that they had it made, yet the opening chapters of Judges paint a sad picture.

The people served the Lord throughout the lifetime of Joshua and of the elders who outlived him and who had seen all the great things the Lord had done for Israel...After that whole generation had been gathered to their fathers, another generation grew up, who knew neither the Lord nor what he had done for Israel. Then the Israelites did evil in the eyes of the Lord and served the Baals. They forsook the Lord, the God of their fathers, who had brought them out of Egypt. They followed and worshipped various gods of the people around them. (Judges 2:7, 10-12)

Pass it on

How did that state of affairs come about? The older generation had forgotten to pass on the endless stories of God's deliverances, miracles, blessings, guidance, provision and victories. In one generation it was all forgotten.

Collective memory is powerful but fades as eyewitnesses die. Oral histories are one way of keeping history alive. Let's realise that there is an emerging generation who didn't experience the events of 1994 when what has become known as the Toronto Blessing swept across churches in Britain.

Every week for several years the church I attended used to have Catch the Fire meetings that were rather wild, all great fun! I remember sitting on the platform steps one night around midnight surrounded by a sea of people. 'One day we will be talking about this!' I said to a friend. So, let's talk.

Then there was the excitement of the charismatic renewal of the 60s and 70s. Yes, there was dancing in the streets 40 years ago! Tell the stories.

Psalm 78:2-4 makes this challenging statement, *'I will utter hidden things, things from of old – what we have heard and known, what our fathers have told us. We will not hide them from their children; we will tell the next generation.'*

There is so much more that can be said about the importance of generational thinking and blessings but that's for later, in chapters 9, 10, and 11.

Everyone likes a good story

Traditional cultures stay alive through stories. They tell the next generation who they are and where they have come from. Stories give identity and destiny.

Today there is a resurgence of interest in Celtic spirituality. The hearth was at the heart of the Celtic home. They had a word for it, *tellach*. It was a place where the family gathered around the fire, not just for meals, but to tell stories. It was seen as a sacred place where there was a meeting of heaven and earth.

It brought the generations together and it's easy to imagine the children listening spellbound to family stories and receiving spiritual teaching as the bannock bread was pulled from the fire and shared around.

The power is in the telling

It's interesting that the word 'gospel' which was chosen to translate the Greek *evangllion* came from the Old English word 'godspell,' which meant 'a good story or spell.' In a sense the gospel stories didn't just cover the three years of Jesus' ministry, but have continued for the last 2000 years as his church has carried on the work of bringing heaven on earth.

As stories are told, they carry with them a certain power. Recalling the histories, is not just giving testimony of what God has done in the past, but exercising our faith that the same things can happen today. Revelation 19:10 says that *'The testimony of Jesus is the spirit of prophecy.'* These stories carry a prophetic declaration that the life of the Spirit that worked in the past can accomplish the same again.
Twenty-first century man is fascinated by history. As we tell the 'family stories' it roots us. For many, life has become a 'style' and reality is a personal construct, with only superficial relationships. A fast-paced world can leave people feeling rootless and searching for meaning.

Even Christians who have their security in Christ need to understand that they are part of the church universal, past and present, with deep, deep roots from which they can draw sustenance and strength for the journey.

The watering hole

Not all memorial stones are as obvious as old chapels. One unlikely 'memorial stone' I know comes in the form of a Saxon chief's burial mound called Taeppa's Mound after which the village of Taplow,

Buckinghamshire is named. But I'm getting ahead of myself. A good friend of mine, Julie, had an idea bubbling up inside of her. It was one of those 'God ideas' that wouldn't go away. She had just come back from a week at Bethel Church, Redding, California where had found herself yelling, 'Revival for Britain!' at the front of one of their meetings. She was stirred to the core of her being and we were walking through the grounds of Clivedon Estate one afternoon talking about it. Together we had a passion to see revival come to Britain.

Julie's vision was for a meeting where those who were passionate about the presence of God could just worship together. It was to be a place of healing and refreshment, and so monthly Sunday evening meetings called 'the Watering Hole' were born. We had some precious times together as the presence of the Holy Spirit would descend on us.

I remember one meeting when there was such a holy presence that no one moved or spoke for at least 45 minutes. By this time our numbers were up to 60 or so. We saw people getting saved and healed. We didn't have much of an agenda, but used to meet together beforehand to share what we felt God was saying.

Taeppa's Mound

It wasn't until after we had been going a few months that Julie began to do some research on the area. She was amazed at what she discovered. A stone's throw away from where we held the meetings, the whole of the southwest of our nation had been won to the Lord through a man called Birinus whose ministry included healings and other miracles. Without knowing any of this our visions were the same, yet spanned one and a half thousand years! It was clear that this was God-orchestrated.

This is the story. (3, 4)

In 633 AD an Italian bishop called Birinus, later St Birinus, was sent as a missionary to England by Pope Honorius. Birinus promised the Pope that he would 'scatter seeds of the holy faith in the remotest regions of England where no teacher had been before.'

Missionaries were instructed not to destroy the pagan sites, but 'redeem them for the Lord' by sprinkling holy water on them and building a church. Birinus found one such site, Taeppa's Mound, prominently placed on a hill overlooking the Thames Valley. A few metres down the hill was a pagan sacred pool.

A nation converted

Here Birinus stood and preached the gospel. Not only were many locals converted, but the king of the West Saxons, Cynegisl, became a Christian. Thus it followed that the whole of the West Anglo-Saxon kingdom were Christianised.

The Saxons were Germanic tribes who had invaded England around 200 years previously. Some had settled in the south and west of England in an area which came to be known as Wessex. This was the same region where Alfred, perhaps one of England's greatest Christian kings, ruled in the 9th century.

Birinus' converts were taken down the hill to the pool to be baptised, and it may be that the king was baptised there too. The pool is still there today and is known as Bapsy Pond. It is continuously filled with water from a spring flowing from where Birinus had the original church built.

Birinus was made bishop of the West Saxons and established an Episcopal see at Dorchester, in what is now Oxfordshire. Tradition tells us of miracles associated with Birinus. You can write them all off as superstition rather than historical fact if you wish, but I think that tradition must be built on at least some truth; there's probably a mixture.

One story is of an old woman who was blind and deaf who had a vision telling her to go to Birinus. He made the sign of the cross over her eyes and ears and she was cured.

Miracles have been recorded that took place at Birinus's shrine. A blind man received sight and a young man deaf and mute from birth both heard and spoke. Lepers were cleansed and it is recorded that the dead were raised.

On the 1,300th anniversary of St Birinus coming to England, a congregation of thousands gathered at Bapsy Pond as the Bishop of Dorchester baptised five babies (it must have been in faith because the water is now a murky green!). Mass choirs gathered in the open air, including one from prestigious Eton College.

Do it again

Following our discovery about the rich heritage of the place, we began to spiritually re-dig the wells. Each month when we met we talked about St Birinus and told some of the stories. We reminded ourselves of the scripture in Habakkuk 3:2, *'Lord, I have heard of your fame; I stand in awe of your deeds, O Lord. Renew them in our day, in our time make them known.'* We prayed for healings, we praised, we worshipped and asked the Lord to 'do it again!'

I love to take visitors to stand on Taeppa's Mound, a place of such spiritual significance which commands an amazing view over the Thames Valley. We pray toward the north, south, east and west that the land and its people in view will once again know the Lord. Talking about places and people of great spiritual and historic significance is one thing, but to pray and worship in the same geographic location is powerful.

Such places such as this exist all over Britain, and all it takes is some research at a local library to unearth God's involvement with our history. Who knows what you may discover, and more importantly, what you might do with it!

Or it may be the other way round. Like Julie, you may feel prompted to hold a celebration or to pray in a specific place, only to find that there are deep spiritual wells to be tapped into.

Caught, not taught

A few years ago I came up with the idea of 'revival trips.' I'm immensely privileged to work in the one-year training programme of River Church in the Thames Valley, west of London. It's one thing to tell the stories of revival history in a classroom situation, but another thing altogether to visit the places of past revivals or historic sites associated with moves of God.

We do one such trip each term, and they have become some of the highlights of the year. Without being too theological about it, as you are physically in a geographic location there is an atmosphere that lingers, a place of presence.

Encountering life

This came home to me when I was researching for a post-graduate degree in the year 2000 which took me to the pages of an old magazine called *Confidence*. (5) From 1908 onwards, its articles, letters and reports told the story of the Pentecostal revival. It was published from the hub of the revival in Britain, the town of Sunderland on the northeast coast.

For several days as I was shut away poring over piles of archived material, I encountered life: *zoe*, the God kind of life which is vibrant and which never dies. I read stories of men and women who were hungry for the same power and presence they had read about in the book of Acts. These were stories of encounter as men and women experienced the baptism of the Holy Spirit and spoke in tongues for the first time. There were testimonies of miraculous healings, deliverances and salvations.

The words in the magazine carried this life. As I turned the pages, I felt I was entering their world; I was feeling their fire, their excitement and passion. My spirit was with them, although I was still in a small room with a pile of papers in front of me. I didn't fully understand this connection with the past that I had made, but it sent me delving into history books. I asked the Holy Spirit to illuminate his word for answers, some of which form the content of this book.

If stories in a book or magazine have this power, how much more so being in a physical location where men and women were actually caught up in revival?

I will be looking at the revivals associated with these places in later chapters but let me tell you about some of the trips and a little of what happened in the locations. You may be inspired to make them yourself. You won't be disappointed, and you may have your own stories to tell.

The Welsh experience

Our first trip of the year is to Moriah Chapel in Loughor, the home of the 1904 Welsh revival. We all set out in a convoy of cars and before visiting Moriah call in at Antioch Church in Loughor for lunch. Like many others, this church is seeking to re-dig the wells of the Welsh Revival.

Today Moriah Chapel is home to a Welsh-speaking congregation. Although small in number, they are well aware of their past history and host visitors from all parts of the world. A young man called Evan Roberts led this revival which lasted 18 months and swept thousands into the kingdom of God, so its influence far outweighed the small principality.

Sitting in the old side chapel which doubled up as a school room, it seems that little has changed since it was packed with men and women, boys and girls who wouldn't go home. In this setting we are told the stories of what happened just over 100 years ago.

Heaven on earth

The *Western Mail*, November 11th 1904, reported,

A remarkable religious revival is now taking place at Loughor. For some days now a young man named Evan Roberts, a native of Loughor, has been causing great surprise at Moriah Chapel. The place has been besieged by dense crowds of people unable to obtain admission. Such excitement has prevailed that the road on which the chapel is situated has been lined with people from end to end... The preacher soon launches out into a fervent, and, at times, impassioned oration. His statements have had stirring effects upon his listeners. Many who have disbelieved Christianity for years are again returning to the fold of their younger days.

One night, so great was the enthusiasm invoked by the young revivalist that, after his sermon which lasted two hours, the vast congregation remained praying and singing until 2.30 in the morning! Shopkeepers are closing early in order to get a place in the chapel, and tin and steel workers throng to the place in their working clothes. (6)

On that particular night Moriah was teeming with over 800 people trying to squeeze into the little chapel. A young girl in her early teens seemed to capture the feeling when she cried out, 'Oh, what will heaven be like if it is so wonderful down here!' (7)

What do we do? We pray. One year we all knelt on the old, frayed carpet and interceded for our nation. Once we gathered round the ancient piano and sang the haunting love song of the Welsh Revival, 'Here is love vast as the ocean...' (8) A few of the more radical among us sneaked round the back to the small graveyard and lay on Evan's grave.

All are impacted in varying ways. Students who previously knew nothing of the revival are gripped by the belief that the same thing can happen in their town.

Bend me

A few hours' drive away is Blaenannerch Calvinistic Methodist Chapel. It is a rather austere and ageing chapel at the side of the road, but it holds a secret.

Before Evan Roberts set Wales ablaze from the meetings at Moriah Chapel, he experienced what he called, 'Blaenannerch's great meeting.'

He was studying for the ministry and heard of some special meetings at Blaenannerch so he went there one Thursday night in September 1904 with a group of friends. At the end of the meeting the visiting speaker, Seth Joshua prayed, 'Bend us, O Lord.' At that moment the Spirit of God fell powerfully on Evan and he cried out for God to 'bend him.' (9)

Evan was never the same again, and led by the Spirit returned to Loughor. The rest, as they say, is history and we will be looking at what happened in chapters 4 to 8.

In Blaenannerch Chapel on a pew to the left side of the pulpit is a small brass plaque indicating where Evan prayed the 'Bend me' prayer. I once took a group of students there and one by one we sat in that place and prayed and prophesied over each other. There were some powerful encounters that day.

The mother church of worldwide Methodism

In the heart of the City of London, in fact in City Road, are some curious street names, Worship Street, Tabernacle Street and Epworth Street. These are clues to the origins of an old house and chapel tucked away back from the busy road and opposite the largest dissenters' grave yard in London, Bun Hill Fields. To mention John Wesley Highwalk among them would give the game away.

This is where we go for our second revival trip of the year. (10)

For the last 13 years of his life John Wesley, who became known as the founder of Methodism, lived and died in this narrow four-storey house next to a chapel he had built. It was his London base.

One of the rooms in the house next to his bedroom is called 'The powerhouse of Methodism' because this is where Wesley could be found on his knees at four am every day. The small kneeler is still there in front of a table where his old Bible sits.

Wesley is buried behind the chapel and a monument marks the spot. In the crypt of the chapel is a museum of Methodism and contains Wesley's original pulpit in which you can stand. Of course we all get our photo taken in the classic revivalist pose, bible held close to the chest by the left hand, with the right hand raised to heaven. (You can do this at Moriah Chapel, too!)

Although Wesley said, 'The world is my parish' and in his lifetime travelled 250,000 miles around Britain, these buildings serve as a reminder of this amazing man of God and the legacy he left this nation.

There is also a side chapel called the Foundry Chapel with pews taken from the Old Foundry, a nearby chapel where Wesley held some of his early meetings. The old organ is here on which Charles Wesley composed many of his 6000 hymns. With permission you can play this.

This year we all stood outside around Wesley's memorial and sang his great hymn, 'And can it be that I should gain, an interest in the Saviour's blood...' ending with a rousing 'My chains fell off, my heart was free, I rose, went forth and followed thee.' (11) The young West African man who showed us round brought life to the story of John Wesley and Methodism in what is now called the mother church of worldwide Methodism.

A heart strangely warmed

Not far away, still in the city, is Aldersgate Street. A large bronze sculpture called the Aldersgate Flame was erected there in 1981 and marks the location of Wesley's conversion experience. On it is inscribed the text from his journal, Wednesday, May 24th 1738: (12)

In the evening I went very unwillingly to a society in Aldersgate Street, where one was reading Luther's preface to the Epistle to the Romans. About a quarter before nine, while the leader was describing the change which God works in the heart through faith in Christ, I felt my heart strangely warmed. I felt I did trust in Christ alone for salvation; and an assurance was given me that He had taken away my sins, even mine, and saved me from the law of sin and death.

Yes, this is written for all to see on the streets of London. Rather like a memorial stone in Canaan!

The Angel of the North

Overlooking the A1 on the approach to Tyneside in the north east of England is an angel. It's visible to any passing motorist as its metal body stands 20 metres tall. The wings are not those that move in obedience to the bidding of God but aeroplane wings which span 54 metres.

They are slightly tilted to create a sense of embrace, but this angel is earthbound.

This modern sculpture was erected in 1998, as a symbol of renewal and hope for what had been a depressed industrial region, especially after the closure of the ship yards and the demise of iron and steel works. However, I believe it has prophetic significance as it hovers over an area with a rich Christian heritage.

The cradle of Christianity

As the A1 continues and parallels the North Sea, a small island comes to view which can only be reached at low tide apart from a boat. Lindisfarne, or Holy Island, (13) is where in AD 635 a small group of monks led by Bishop Aidan built a small wooden monastery and set out to re-evangelise the kingdom of Northumbria.

For sixteen years they walked the lanes, talked to the ordinary people and established Christian communities. Once Northumberland was re-converted, Aidan and his monks continued south to Mercia (now known as the Midlands of England), then south east to East Anglia and Essex.

Cuthbert was a later travelling, evangelising bishop from Lindisfarne, a charismatic figure who we'll be looking at in the next chapter. He was a man of prayer whose ministry was characterised by the miraculous.

Christianity is in the foundations of Northumberland and it is rightly called 'the cradle of Christianity.' As one of the main gateways of Christianity into Britain, it's interesting that according to the 2001 census there is a higher percentage of Christians in the North East of England than anywhere else in Britain (80.1%).(14) History shows us that the people of Northumberland have been especially receptive and embracing of revivals.

This is where we go for our third and longest revival trip, taking in a visit to St Peter's Church in Sunderland, one of the oldest churches in Britain. We also visit All Saints' Sunderland, home of the 20th century Pentecostal revival in Britain and its parish hall where most of the revival meetings were held. This is now the home of Monkwearmouth Christian Fellowship, an Elim Pentecostal Church.

A thin place

As you drive across the causeway that links Holy Island with the mainland, you feel you are entering another world. The quaint streets speak of days gone by, and the attractive seascape is breathtaking. However there is something else in the very atmosphere that sets it apart.

Holy Island is a centre for Celtic spirituality, and the Celts have a phrase which captures this exactly, a 'thin place.' A thin place is where the veil between heaven and earth is especially thin, where the presence of God is tangible. Lindisfarne is more than visiting a ruined priory or tracing its history in the museum. It's breathing in the presence of God as the wind gently blows and a place where it's easy just to 'be.'

This is captured by an old Celtic blessing:

Deep peace of the running wave
Deep peace of the flowing air
Deep peace of the quiet earth
Deep peace of the shining stars
Deep peace of the Son of Peace.

Releasing life

It's also a place of inspiration where in the past the Holy Spirit has stirred the hearts of men to win the nation. These few monks made great inroads into the heartland of England with none of the modern communications we have today. They moved out because of passion and relied on the Spirit of God to lead them.

Our two days on the island were a time for personal reflection and for hearing what the Holy Spirit wanted to say to our nation. One evening we stood by the still water of the bay with the shores of the mainland in the distance, and released words of life over Britain. What better place to do it?

It was as if we were standing in the same line of the monks all those years ago, which in reality we were. Yes, we looked a motley group as we pointed and spoke over the sea, but I'm sure God was pleased.

The glory of kings

It's worth some digging in a library, it's worth exploring the web, it's worth seeking out senior believers, and it's worth the effort. It's worth taking a journey to a place of past blessing. It may cost you, but it's worth it. Ask the Holy Spirit to guide you. Proverbs 25:2 says, *'It is the glory of God to conceal a matter; to search out a matter is the glory of kings.'*

As Christians we are all kings and by definition have a royal inheritance. But we can't inherit until we know what it is, and what hidden riches are ours by right. We are not under the laws of 'treasure trove,' but God gives us freely 'the riches of his glorious inheritance in the saints' (Ephesians 1:18).

Not just Britain

This book is written using examples from British history, but the principles and ideas are transferable whether you are reading in Brighton or Boston, Southend or Sydney. Britain shares so much history with the New World, and in many cases our Christian roots have the same origins.

Wherever or whoever you are, the Lord promises:

I will give you the treasures of darkness, riches stored in secret places,
so that you may know that I am the Lord, the God of Israel who
summons you by name.
Isaiah 45:3

End notes

1. Judith Hunter, *Tough Assignment*, Eton Wick Methodist Chapel, UK, 1986.
2. Colin Whittaker, *Great Revivals*, Marshall Morgan and Scott, Basingstoke, UK, 1884, p 65.
3. Eric Fitch, *Unknown Taplow*, Windsor Publications, Windsor, UK, 1988.
4. Bede, *The Ecclesiastical History of the English People*, Oxford University Press, Oxford, UK, 2008, pp 119-20.
5. Original copies of *Confidence* (1908–1926) are held in the Donald Gee Centre, Mattersey Hall Bible College, Mattersey, Doncaster, UK.
6. Rick Joyner, *The World Aflame*, Morning Star Publications, Charlotte, NC, USA, 1993, pp 48-9.
7. Ibid., p 49.
8. *Here is Love*, William Rees, 1876.
9. Kevin Adams, *A Diary of Revival*, CWR, Farnham, UK, 2004, p 67.
10. www.wesleyschapel.org.uk
11. Charles Wesley, *And Can It Be*, 1738.
12. www.methodistheritage.org.uk/aldersgate.htm
13. The name Holy Island was given to Lindisfarne after the Norman Conquest

(1066) by the monks in Durham who looked back over the island's 'holy history'.

14. www.news.bbc.co.uk/2/shared/spl/hi/uk/03/census_2001/html/religion.stm

2
In the Foundations

'The English by outward miracles are turned to inward grace.'
(quoted in Bede's *Ecclesiastical History of the English People,* (1)
referring to the ministry of St Augustine)

For three years of my life I lived in Canterbury, Kent, while I was studying at what is now Christ Church University. Canterbury Cathedral is the mother church of the worldwide Anglican Communion, and towers majestically over the quaint narrow streets of the old city. Almost every day I would walk through the cathedral precincts and pass St Martin's Church and St Augustine's Abbey on the way to my lectures.

St Martin's Church is the oldest church in Britain and dates back to Roman times. Canterbury Cathedral was founded by St Augustine in the sixth century when he came to re-evangelise the British. And at the time I was not in the least interested!

I was a Pentecostal, which in those days still stood apart from mainstream Christianity, although it was the era of the Charismatic Renewal and times were changing. It meant that my thinking was rather separatist. These old buildings and stories of saints smacked of religion, and in my mind were totally irrelevant to a present move of the Holy Spirit.

Although I didn't realise it at the time, this was nothing but a spiritual elitism and arrogance on my part, born out of ignorance. How I've changed! I now see them as part of a rich Christian heritage in this country which needs to be embraced and cherished.

What a strategy!

Can you imagine if in our nation today thousands were coming to Christ because of all the miracles that were happening? We'd call it a revival, wouldn't we?

This was St Augustine's mission strategy, albeit unplanned, and it worked! Four years after Augustine arrived in England, Pope Gregory felt it necessary to write him a letter warning him not to become proud because of all the miracles he performed. In his letter he acknowledged, 'The English by outward miracles are drawn to inward grace,' not just by preaching the word. (2) What an amazing phrase, and surely a strategy that we would say a loud 'Amen' to today.

Words are so powerful and these words written years ago still ring true down the ages. 'Outward miracles' and 'inward grace' are in the foundations of our nation. Was it ever meant to change? Let this thought capture your hearts.

The bedrock of Britain

The people we are going to read about in this chapter walked in the light they had. It's so easy in the 21st century, with the benefit of years of Christian history, to write off some of their practices and beliefs as plain bizarre. Of course our context is vastly different, and we need to take a hermeneutical approach as we read the histories taking their context and worldview into account.

Biographies of saints and miracles written with an uncritical and unreflective approach are called 'hagiography,' but in many cases these are the only sources we have. These were ordinary men and women who because of their passion and encounters with God gave their lives to bring the gospel to Britain.

That is a good enough reason to give them honour. They weren't perfect, but then neither are we! They laid the foundations of Christianity in our nation, which are the bedrock of Britain.

Enter the Romans

I've often wondered when Christianity arrived in Britain. The answer is, much earlier than I thought! Stick with the history... Julius Caesar led the first Roman forays to Britain in 55 BC, although Britain did not become a Roman province until AD 33 under Claudius Caesar. Where the Roman armies went, the merchants and artisans followed, using the extensive system of Roman roads that acted like arteries into the occupied territories.

On the opposite end of the Roman world was the provincial backwater of Judea where Jesus lived and was crucified in AD 33. Thoughts, ideas and new religions travelled along trade routes, so it would be inconceivable that stories about Jesus were not known in Britain. One obvious sailing route from the Mediterranean was around Spain and France and into the Bristol Channel. This links with the tradition that Glastonbury in Somerset is the oldest Christian centre in Britain.

In Acts 2:5, it says that there were *'God-fearing Jews'* from every nation under heaven in Jerusalem. Perhaps there were also visitors from Britain, there for trading purposes rather than for the feast of Pentecost, witnessing these events?

I don't know about you, but I find it a fascinating idea that there are parallel events in Judea and Britain. This Claudius who ruled Britain was the same Claudius mentioned in Acts 11:28 and 18:2. He even named his son Britannicus.

The first martyrs

So Christianity took root in Britain, but because there was 'no other God but Caesar,' Christians were persecuted. The worst persecutions took place under Emperor Diocletian (AD 284-305).

At this time, Alban became the first English martyr (St Albans, a town north of London was named after him), and Aaron and Julius the first Welsh to be martyred in Caerleon near Newport. Christians had to hide in woods and caves, and churches were burnt. However, churches were rebuilt and Christianity was sufficiently established to send three bishops to the Council of Arles in AD 314.

The big turnaround came in AD 312 when Constantine, who was a Christian, became Emperor of Rome (he happened to be in York, England, at the time), and all persecution ended after the Edict of Milan in AD 313. Then in AD 380 Christianity became the official religion of the Empire, and the faith became increasingly institutionalized.

Fact or fiction

Evidence can be found in all sorts of documents for a British church even as early as AD 37. A Welsh monk and historian, Gildas (AD 516-

570) wrote, 'These islands received the beams of light, that is, the holy precepts of Christ, the true sun at the latter part, *as we know*, of the reign of Tiberius Caesar' (AD 14-37). (3)

Whether his sources were correct we don't know, but we can compare them with the writings of Dorotheus, Bishop of Tyre (AD 303) who said, 'Aristobulus, whom Paul saluted when writing in the book of Romans, was Bishop of Britain. Simon Zelotes preached Christ... [and] was crucified in Britannia...' (4)

The Jewish historian Eusebius was his pupil, and so it's not surprising that he wrote, 'The apostles passed beyond the ocean to the isles called the Britannic Isles.' (5)

It seems that the earliest confirmed written evidence for Christianity in Britain is by the church father, Tertullian (AD 200) who wrote, 'all the limits of the Spains, and the diverse nations of the Gauls, and the haunts of the Britons, inaccessible to the Romans, but subjugated to Christ.' (6)

Fact or fiction, stories abound. Even Bede who wrote the definitive *Ecclesiastical History of the English People* mentions a legendary king of Britain, Lucius, receiving the Christian faith as early as AD 156. (7) If you find this all as fascinating as I do, this will give you places to start a search.

We do know, however, that very early on Christianity was becoming global. There's one quote that has a ring of truth about it, 'From India to Britain, all nations resound with the death and resurrection of Christ' (St Jerome, AD 378). (8)

Abandoned, but not by God!

The Romans left Britain in AD 410. Over a period of around a hundred and fifty years, various tribes, the Saxons, Angles and Jutes invaded and terrorized the nation. There were also invasions from Picts in the north and Scots from Ireland as well as internal unrest. Christianity declined and was driven to the western margins of Wales and Cornwall.

However, there were some bright periods, including the arrival of bishops from the continent in AD 429:

Britain was soon filled with the fame of these apostolic bishops. They preached the word of God daily, not only in the churches but also in the streets and the fields... Like the apostles they acquired honour and authority for themselves through a good conscience, their learning through the scriptures and the power of working miracles. (9)

The venerable Bede

Bede's told us so much about the first 700 years of Christianity in Britain in his magnificent book, *The Ecclesiastical History of the English People* (10) which has been translated into modern English. Please don't let the title put you off! I can't tell you how blessed you will be if you do what I did.

Read it with a highlighter pen in your hand and highlight every supernatural occurrence. There are stories of miracles of nature, creative miracles, healings, deliverances, visions, dreams and angelic visitations on page after page. It chronicles the advance of Christianity in this nation in a way which is truly inspiring.

It's a remarkable achievement for a 7th –8th century monk who lived in the monasteries of Jarrow and Wearmouth in the North East of England from the age of seven. It clearly shows that the worldview at the time was comfortable with the miraculous, despite this being at variance with the later rationalism of modernity.

Yes, Bede selected his material like any historian does. The miracles he writes about are based on eye-witness accounts and 'common report,' so cannot be objectively substantiated. Personally, I like to read about the coming of Christianity to Britain with an open heart and mind.

From north and south

Bede calls it 'an unspeakable crime' that [the Christians in Britain] never preached the faith to the Saxons or Angles who inhabited Britain with them. (11) As in the time of the Judges, *'they followed and worshipped various gods of the people around them'* (Judges 2:12).

By the mid-sixth century, Britain was in need of re-evangelization and it came in two directions, from the north and from the south. The two types of Christianity were very different. The Celtic stream flowed into Britain from Ireland via Scotland, and the other was brought by missionaries sent by the Roman Church.

The first great missionary

Patrick was a Welsh lad from a Christian family who was taken by raiders to become a slave in Ireland. His faith grew during this difficult time and with God's help he escaped to France. Once again back home he had his own 'Macedonian call.'

In a dream he heard voices calling, 'Please, holy boy, come and walk among us again.' (12) He said that their cry pierced his heart and so in AD 432 he landed back in Ireland.

What happened next can only be called a series of 'power encounters.' In coming up against pagan religion, Patrick didn't rely on words only but 'proved himself to be a mightier druid than the pagan druids.' (13) After 15 years, Ireland had been evangelized. He had planted 200 churches and baptized 100,000 converts.

This was at a time when a monastic form of Christianity was emerging that took Ireland by storm. It was born in the deserts of Egypt and Syria out of a reaction against a corrupt and institutional church. These monasteries became centres of learning and missionary bases from which the re-evangelization of Britain and indeed Europe began. This was the beginning of what we know as Celtic Christianity.

Their hearts set on pilgrimage

To show their devotion to God, many of these Irish monks set out on a pilgrimage which meant leaving their homeland forever. In AD 563 Columba and a group of monks landed on the Scottish island of Iona and buried their boat on the beach. Columba had already founded some 300 monasteries in Ireland, and their small community of beehive huts became a monastic base for reaching out to the rest of Scotland.

Like Patrick before him, Columba moved in the miraculous. His biographer who wrote *The Life of Columba*, used three main headings: prophesies, miracles and the appearance of angels!(14)

Mission impossible

As a child, Oswald, the king of Northumbria had become a Christian at Iona. Now he wanted his nation to follow him in the faith, so he sent for some monks to come and re-evangelize them. The first attempt failed because the chosen monk, Cornan, thought the English were like barbarians. He declared it an impossible task and impatiently went back to Iona.

What a missed opportunity! Another monk said he should have been more gentle and patient, and so it was that Aidan talked himself into a job. In time he became the man known as 'the apostle of the English.'

In AD 635 Aidan was made a bishop and with twelve volunteers was sent off to Northumbria to try again. King Oswald offered him the choice of anywhere in his kingdom for a monastery and he chose Lindisfarne. This is the tidal island often called Holy Island, just off the coast, which featured in my first chapter.

Mission possible

The first thing the monks did was to have forty days of prayer and fasting to cleanse the land from evil. Aidan then began a school to train local boys to be English leaders of an English church. Many of these boys carried the faith and won other English kingdoms to Christ.

Then Aidan began the main work of his life, the conversion of pagans to Christianity. His strategy was simple, to walk the lanes and talk to the people, so he and the monks set about learning English, the language of the common people.

This is how Bede describes Aidan's mission:

...He and his followers lived as he taught. He never sought or cared for any worldly possessions, and loved to give away to the poor who chanced to meet him whatever he received from kings or wealthy folk.

Whether in town or country, he always travelled on foot unless compelled by the necessity to ride; and whatever people he met on his walks, whether high or low, he stopped and spoke to them. If they were heathen, he urged them to be baptized; and if they were Christians, he strengthened their faith and inspired them by word and deed to live a good life and to be generous to others.(15)

And so Northumbria was converted to faith in Christ. The seeds that Aidan sowed have continued to bear fruit down the centuries.

A child of God in every beggar

Although miracles are attributed to Aidan, it's his passion for God and his character that stands out. This story gives us a clue to Aidan's success. (16)

King Oswin of Deira, a kingdom south of Northumbria, gave Aidan one of his own best horses because he was concerned that he went everywhere on foot. Later on, Aidan met a beggar who asked him for alms, so Aidan gave him the horse complete with saddle and bridle.

Oswin wasn't very pleased and said that if he had known Aidan was going to give the horse to a beggar, he would have given him a poorer quality horse. Aidan challenged him, 'Which is more valuable to you, the son of a mare or a son of God?' Humbly the king agreed he was right.

Aidan was able to see a potential child of God in every beggar. He wanted to be on their level, showing them that Jesus had come as a human to this earth and could identify with them. No wonder he won the hearts of the people.

Cuthbert's angels

One night in AD 651 a 17-year-old English boy called Cuthbert was on the hills in Northumbria looking after sheep when he saw a moving light in the sky. He identified this as a group of angels coming to earth, and he saw them return to heaven with a bright human soul. That was the night Aidan died.

After this encounter, Cuthbert became a monk and eventually went up the ranks to become the sixth bishop of Lindisfarne.

Bede says that angels would often appear and talk to him. There are more stories of healings associated with Cuthbert than any other British saint, many of which were told to Bede by eye witnesses. He moved in all of the spiritual gifts and Bede, in relating one story, quaintly says he had 'a sudden attack of second sight'! We would of course call this prophecy or a word of knowledge.

And miracles...

Cuthbert's reputation for healing meant that many people made the walk across the sand at low tide to Lindisfarne to be prayed for by him. He was a man of compassion and 'no one had to take back the burden he came with.'(17) There are stories of mental, physical, and emotional healings, and of deliverance from demons as well as stories of power over nature.

Space won't allow me to tell all the stories and I hope the reader will look them up. Many are found in another of Bede's books, *The Life of Cuthbert*.(18) I can't resist telling one story of when he was just a boy.

Looking out to sea he saw some monks who had been swept out on a raft during a gale. They had been ferrying logs down the River Tyne and now were in danger of drowning. On one bank of the Tyne some fellow monks were praying for their safety, but on the other bank were a group of jeering locals who hoped they would drown because they didn't like the Christians.

Cuthbert was on the same bank as the hostile crowd and knelt down alone and prayed. The wind changed immediately and the rafts floated back to shore. The crowd was speechless! Bede said that one of the crowd told this story to a large audience and a monk in that audience told it to him.(19)

Loving the people, devoted to God

In the footsteps of Aidan, Cuthbert was a travelling, evangelizing bishop (although at times he did use a horse). He not only covered the length and breadth of Northumbria but also ventured into unevangelized parts of Scotland. Wherever he went, he preached and performed miracles of healing and loved the people.

Although he was a 'people person,' there was a deep desire within him to live alone and be with God. He did so for 10 years, first on the tiny St Cuthbert's Isle accessible only at low tide from Lindisfarne, and then on the nearby Farne Islands. Still the people came.

Being a hermit is foreign to our 21st century thinking, but in those days it was not just a passive withdrawal from the world. It was taking up the task of a front-line soldier engaging in spiritual warfare against the forces of evil, by prayer and fasting.

Miracles are associated with visits to many saints' tombs, but in Cuthbert's case the story goes a stage further. Eleven years after his death his bones were 'elevated' for sainthood and the story goes that they found a fully clothed, undecomposed body. Make of that what you will. If nothing else, that guaranteed his sainthood!

Jan's story

We will all have our own responses to these stories, from being generally inspired to an engagement leading to a spiritual encounter. Jan's story is one such encounter from our last trip to Lindisfarne.

One morning I went down to the sea to pray and looked over the little island where St Cuthbert used to visit to spend time with God. Hearing what I thought were wild geese, I remembered that this was the Celtic symbol for the Holy Spirit. I felt a deep stirring in my heart of the wild Holy Spirit calling to me.

Then the church bells tolled announcing the Eucharist – a calling that echoed throughout the centuries, a calling to community and to worship together. I felt I was receiving a fresh call to live a life of wildness in the Spirit, but expressed through the context of a worshipping community.

The following day I returned to that spot and felt a pull to go over to the island. The tide was receding so I clambered over the seaweed-covered stones and across the tracts of water that lay between me and my destination.

A wooden cross had been placed at the highest point on the island and I stood with arms outstretched with my back to the cross and looked over the wide expanse of sea to the mainland. From there I prayed a blessing on my country. Then I heard the calling sound again which I had thought was the wild geese, but in fact was wild seals.

I heard the voice of that wild Spirit speak to me again, 'This is my calling to you – to take risks, to stand in the shadow of my cross, to reach out with blessing to the community, and I will bring to you those who I need you to love in my name.'

I felt it had been no mistake that I had misidentified the sound – for surely the presence of the Holy Spirit is calling out from the very people he brings to us, and in loving them, we are loving him.

It was a significant moment of confirming the calling on my life, so I laid another stone on the cairn that was built there as a witness to that moment.

The age of saints

The sixth and seventh centuries in Britain could be called 'the age of saints.' There were far more men and women of God than we can give credit to in these pages. Each has their own story and contribution to Britain's spiritual foundations, and in many cases have been immortalised in place names and churches dedicated to them.

Cornwall is a good example of this. Welsh missionary monk St David evangelized Wales and southwest England. St Ninian was a missionary among the Picts of Scotland. The list goes on...most were from the Celtic stream of Christianity but there were some exceptions like St Birinus, sent independently from Augustine and who played such a significant role in Britain's re-evangelisation.

Power encounters

The gods of the nations are idols, but the Lord made the heavens. (Psalm 96:5)

Patrick faced the druids in Ireland and showed his God to be more powerful, winning their king to the faith. Columba won the king of the Picts through a demonstration of power over a storm. Aidan felt it necessary to cleanse the land of Lindisfarne from evil, while monks and hermits such as Cuthbert fought spiritual battles against the powers of darkness on behalf of peoples and nations.

All this is reminiscent of the power encounter between Elijah and the prophets of Baal on Mount Carmel (1 Kings 18) and an integral part of their missionary strategy. In Acts we see that power encounters helped the gospel progress and a 'warfare worldview' was maintained by these Christians who laid our foundations. Like Paul, they didn't just use *'wise and persuasive words'* but added *'a demonstration of the Spirit's power'* (1 Corinthians 2:4).

Faces of Angles

Bede tells a story(20) which is said to have prompted the re-evangelization of Britain by Rome in AD 597. Before he became pope, Gregory was in a market in Rome where amongst other goods were some boys for sale as slaves. They had 'fair complexions, handsome faces and lovely hair,' and Gregory was so taken by them that he asked where they were from.

He was told they came from the island of Britain and he further enquired whether the islanders were Christian. By now paganism once again had a hold on Britain and on hearing this, Gregory gave a deep sigh and said, 'Alas that the author of darkness should have men so bright of face in his grip, and that minds so devoid of inward grace should bear so graceful an outward form.'

He was told that they were from the race called *Angli*. 'Good', he replied, 'They have the face of angels and such men should be fellow heirs of the angels in heaven.' Further inquiry told him that they were from Deira, a kingdom in the North East whose king was Aelle. In another play on words he said, 'De ira, snatched from the wrath of Christ and called to his mercy...Alleluia! The praise of God the creator must be sung in those parts.'

Gregory asked the pope to send missionaries to the Angles to convert them to Christ and so it was that Augustine and 40 monks landed in Kent as an answer to that request. From the perspective of Rome, we were 'the ends of the earth' at that time!

The Kent connection

The county of Kent in the south east of England is the part of Britain nearest to the continent. Its king was Ethelbert who was married to Bertha, a Christian princess, so the little evangelizing party felt sure of a warm welcome. Bertha had restored St Martin's, a church in Canterbury that dated from Roman times, which is still used for worship. St Augustine based himself there and it became Mission England HQ.

Bede wrote,

In this church they first began to meet, to chant the psalms, to pray, to say Mass, to preach, and to baptise, until when the king had been converted to the faith they received greater liberty to preach everywhere and to build or restore churches. (21)

In due course Ethelbert was converted and so were many of his subjects, so many tens of thousands, in fact, that on Christmas Day AD 597 there were mass baptisms. There was probably a remnant of Christians left in Kent from Roman times.

Augustine founded an abbey close to the church (its ruins are still there) and a school, and by AD 604 bishops had been sent to London and Rochester. The king gave him land to build Canterbury Cathedral.

More mass baptisms

One of Augustine's monks, Paulinus, accompanied Ethelbert's daughter Ethelberga as her personal chaplain when she married Edwin, the first Christian king of Northumbria in AD 616. Paulinus became bishop of York and through him the Christian faith spread into Yorkshire,

Lincolnshire and Nottinghamshire, so that there were mass baptisms in the local rivers. Hild, or Hilda, was one lady he baptized.

St Hilda

No story about the beginnings of Christianity in Britain would be complete without the mention of women. So far we have emphasised men, but there was a place for women within Celtic Christianity and many founded monasteries. Both Aidan and Cuthbert promoted women leaders.

Hild (22), who was from a royal background, knew Aidan who gave her some land just north of the River Wear and persuaded her to establish a small community. She moved on to Hartlepool and then to Whitby, still on the northeast coast of England.

In both places she was abbess of double monasteries where nuns and monks were in community together. She trained both men and women, and five of her students became bishops. We are told by Bede that she was sought out by ordinary people and kings because of her wisdom.

One historian said of Hild, 'No woman in the Middle Ages ever held a position comparable with that of Hild of Whitby.'(23) A strong woman, (her name meant 'battle') she was just one of several outstanding Celtic Christian women leaders of her day.

Songwriter and poet

This story puts worship firmly into the foundations of Britain. It's all about a young, illiterate cow herder called Caedmon (24) who became the first Christian, English singer-songwriter and poet.

Each night after looking after the cows the men would entertain themselves, taking it in turns playing a harp and singing. However, Caedmon couldn't sing and used to go home. One night instead of going home, he went to the cow shed to sleep and he had a dream that would change his life.

In the dream someone stood by him and called him by name, 'Caedmon, sing me something...sing about the beginning of creation.' He began to sing songs he had never heard, all of which praised the God of creation. When he woke up, he remembered what he had sung in his dream and added more verses.

Caedmon was actually 'discovered' by Hild because he worked in her community. After he went and told her what had happened, she gave him a little test. She told him a Bible story and asked him to come back the next day with the story made into a song, and he did so.

Hild was so taken with him that she invited him to join the monastery to put scriptural stories into songs and poems in everyday English. His songs and poems were inspirational and helped many ordinary people enjoy the Bible. Caedmon was a seventh century worship leader indeed!

The two meet

These two missionary endeavours, the Celtic and Roman, were different in attitude, outlook and organization. The Celtic variety of Christianity had developed under missionaries from Ireland and was separate from Rome. It centred on abbeys and monasteries led by abbots, whereas Roman Christianity was led by bishops from ecclesiastical centres in towns.

Missionary tactics were different too. The Celts first related to the common people, whereas the Roman way of doing things was to convert the king and his subjects would follow. When Augustine came, he brought with him gifts and letters to the Celtic church trying to persuade them to come under his authority, but they resisted.

In AD 644 there was a meeting or synod of the two streams at Whitby on the north east coast which was presided over by Hild. A verdict was found in favour of Rome. The Irish monks left Lindisfarne and Cuthbert moved in on the scene as Prior. Celtic Christianity was again pushed to the western margins of Britain.

A spirituality for our times

The spirituality of the Celts fits very well with our post-modern worldview. As life gets more frenetic, the draw to their simplicity is appealing. The Celts had a love and respect for all creation and with that came a blurring of the sacred and secular.

They saw themselves as bringers of blessing, releasing the shalom of heaven to earth. They were hospitable and had a concern for the poor and needy. God was seen as a good God who could be encountered. They were deeply contemplative yet missional. The miraculous was part of their lives...and so much more.

I like that. I like living in the 21st century too, but these are some values that we can embrace. Lindisfarne, Holy Island has been bathed in this spirituality for a one and a half millennia. No wonder the Holy Spirit is in the air you breathe, and 'God encounters' just happen.

Let Britain rejoice!

God has been so good to our little island. Through the vicissitudes of invasion, conflict, internal unrest and persecution that accompanied the first 700 years of Christianity in Britain, the light of the gospel went out. Though sometimes nearly extinguished, the flames spread until Bede could write that every kingdom professed the gospel of Christ.

Bede ends his history with the words, 'Let the earth rejoice in his perpetual kingdom and let Britain rejoice in his faith and let the multitudes of isles be glad and give thanks at the remembrance of his holiness.' (25) Amen!

Such is the story of what was laid in our foundation as a nation and this is God's promise to us:

You shall raise up the foundations of many generations.
Isaiah 58:12 (NKJV)

Endnotes

1. Bede, *The Ecclesiastical History of the English People*, Oxford University Press, Oxford, UK, 2008, op. cit., 1.32., p 58. (written AD 735)
2. Ibid., 1.32, 2.1., p 58, 69.
3. Gildas, *De Exidio Brittaniae*, Sec. 8, p 25, AD 550, quoted in http://www. goodshepherdaoc/Anglican/Tradition.html
4. Dorotheus, *Synopsis de Apostol*, Synop. 9. 'Simon Zelotes', quoted ibid.
5. Eusebius, *De Demonstratione Evangelii*, Lib iii, quoted ibid.
6. Tertullian, *Tutullian Def. Fidei*, p 179, quoted ibid.
7. Bede, op.cit., 1.4., p 14.
8. Jerome, *Epistd, xiii, ad Paulinum*, quoted in http://www.christianjudiasm. com/christianity_in_the_4th_century.htm
9. Bede, op. cit., 1.17., p 30.
10. Bede, op. cit.
11. Bede, op. cit., 1.22., p 36.
12. Ruth Tucker, *From Jerusalem to Irian Jaya*, Zondervan, Grand Rapids, Michigan, USA, 1983, p 39.
13. Ibid., p 39.
14. Kate Tristram, *The Story of Holy Island*, Canterbury Press, Norwich, UK,

2009, p 13.

15. Bede, op. cit., 3.5., pp 116-7.

16. Tristram, op. cit., p 26.

17. Cuthbert, Marygate House, Lindisfarne, Information booklet, p 10.

18. Bede's Life of Cuthbert is included in J. F. Webb, Eddius Stephanus, David Hugh, *Age of Bede*, Penguin, UK, 1998.

19. Cuthbert, Information Booklet, op.cit., p 5-6.

20. Bede, op.cit,. 2.1., pp 70-71.

21. Bede, op.cit., 1.26., pp 40-41.

22. Bede, op.cit., 4.23., pp 210-14.

23. F.M. Stenton, *Anglo Saxon England*, Oxford University Press, Oxford, UK, 1971, pp 161-2.

24. Bede, op.cit., 4.24., p 215-7.

25. Bede, op.cit., 5.23., p 290.

3
So Many Rivers

'I am verily persuaded the Lord hath more truth and light yet to break forth from his holy word.' *Farewell speech of John Robinson, leader of the Pilgrim Fathers,1620* (1)

Christian branding

The perceptions of visitors to Britain are interesting. Several years ago a Ugandan friend visited us for the first time and when I asked him how he liked it here, he said, 'Your country has so many rivers!' This was an observation I would never have considered. Thinking about his response, I felt it was prophetic.

Over the years there have been many moves of God and discoveries of 'new' truths which have resulted in the formation of denominations. These are sometimes referred to as streams or rivers, each having their own flavour of Christianity. Most countries have their fair share, and Britain is no different.

In our villages, towns and cities, we are confronted with church or chapel buildings that come in all shapes and sizes and states of repair or disrepair. Some are welcoming and some decidedly unfriendly looking.

Usually outside is a notice board which not only gives the times of services, activities and the name of the minister, but advertises its brand, or to use ecclesiastical language, denomination. Baptist, Methodist, the Society of Friends, Church of England, Congregational, Presbyterian, Brethren, United Reformed, Pentecostal...the list goes on.

To the average non-churchgoer, these titles mean relatively little and just add to their confusion about Christianity. So how did this state of affairs come about? That's what we will be looking at in this chapter.

The source is heaven

If you think about any river, it has a source. All rivers begin as springs from underground, and as they bubble up they are fed by numerous tributaries and swollen by rainfall. If you trace this scenario back to the beginning, all the water they contain came from the same source, rain; some has just been stored millions of years in underground chambers or rivers.

So the rivers of different denominations ultimately have the source of their life in heaven. Rather than see denominations as sectarian strongholds, let's see them as historical manifestations of the work of the Holy Spirit in the earth and celebrate their creativity and diversity.

It's easy to write off denominations as divisive but when you begin to explore their beginnings you find that many were born in revival or centred round a newly discovered truth. Frequently there was a charismatic figure or group whose heart beat with heaven. It's just that what was bubbling in them couldn't be contained in the existing church structures.

Prophetic voices

On the day of Pentecost (Acts 2) the Holy Spirit was poured out on everyone, regardless of gender, age and social class. Sons and daughters would prophesy, young men would see visions and old men dream dreams; all were given a voice. In the Spirit, freedom was granted from the enslaving order and a free people always spell danger in the eyes of those who seek to control.

Down through history these prophetic voices have challenged the religious status quo and often have been ridiculed, at worst, martyred for their faith. Movements of the Spirit have been legislated against and their existence threatened; Spirit-filled believers have been exiled and imprisoned. But the price they paid built on the spiritual foundations we read about in the last chapter, and made a way for the freedom we have today.

Still more light

John Robinson, who led the Pilgrim Fathers onto the Mayflower in 1620 as they sailed to the New World, said, 'I am verily persuaded the Lord hath more truth and light yet to break forth from His holy Word.'(2) He was a radical Baptist who had been forced to live in Holland because his views did not conform to those of the established Church of England.

Men and women like him were called Independents, Dissenters or Separatists because they believed in a 'gathered church' where the bond between them was faith in Jesus Christ rather than belonging to an institution. Following the Protestant reformation in 1517, there were many such groups who read the newly translated scripture in the English language with open hearts and minds.

The Spirit shed new light on his word, new revelations unfolded and they began to walk in them. John Robinson got it right; this is what is meant to happen. The truth always sets men free.

Revelation belongs to us all

The word of God is full of treasures to be discovered. Deuteronomy 29:29 says, *'The secret things belong to the Lord our God, but the things revealed belong to us and to our children forever, that we may follow all the words of the law.'*

The light of the Holy Spirit on the word of God births revelation. Gems of truth are not just to be contained in one particular day or age, but are for all believers at all times to embrace. As one old Pentecostal put it, truths are there 'slumbering in the Word' (3) until they are awakened and then they belong to us.

Martin Luther, the monk who sparked the Reformation in 1517, had a scriptural revelation that *'the just shall live by faith'* (Habakkuk 2:4, Romans 1:17) and not works. His intention was for this to reform the existing Roman church, not produce Protestantism and subsequently a plethora of new denominations. The revelation was meant to belong to everybody and embraced.

Two and a half centuries later, John Wesley's rediscovery of the truth of salvation by faith through grace alone, had the same results. Wesley never intended to start the Methodist denomination. In fact, in 1777, he commented on the different revival movements since the Reformation and in his view their impact was greatly lessened because they had separated from the established church.

Ironically he said, 'But it is not so in this present revival of religion. The Methodists...know their calling...they weighed the matter...and... determined to continue in the church.'(4) But the church did not want them.

Gathered around truth

In the initial stages of new movements people gathered round newly discovered truths or revelations led by charismatic figures such as 17th century George Fox, founder of the Religious Society of Friends, or Quakers, who moved in great anointing. Their Christianity was experiential and a high value was placed on calling, gifting and anointing, resulting in explosions of salvations and spiritual gifts.

Sociologists call this the charismatic phase of a religious movement. The emphasis is on 'getting the job done,' rather than on the person who is doing it. Old prejudices are overcome. Fox's co-leader and later his wife, Margaret Fell, wrote the first book in defence of women leaders and preachers. It was called *Women's Speaking Justified, Proved and Allowed by the Scriptures* (1666) in a day when women had very limited public roles.

Women, Wesley and Whitefield

God raised up prominent female preachers and teachers in the wake of John Wesley's mid-18th century revival gatherings. Willing to follow the Holy Spirit rather than the prevailing culture, he declared, 'If God uses women in the conversion of sinners, who am I that I should withstand God?'(5)

One female preacher was even compared to George Whitefield. Mary Fletcher did for Methodism what Margaret Fell did for the Quakers, in writing the first defence for Methodist women preachers.

Another remarkable lady who was one of the most active and influential leaders in Methodism, used her position to promote Wesley and Whitefield. She was Selina, Countess of Huntingdon, and was a patron to her own denomination, 'the Countess of Huntingdon's Connexion.' By 1828 there were 200 'Connexion' chapels and although not well known, some 30 remain today.

Organism to organisation

However more often than not, what began in the Spirit does not continue in the Spirit. As the first generation of a movement passes or the founding father dies, so the revelation tends to be 'kept alive' by rules and structure. A living, breathing organism becomes a rigid organisation. Legalism replaces life; human control replaces Holy Spirit flow. In sociological terms, the movement has become institutionalised.

Wesleyan and Primitive Methodism

Within 16 years of Wesley's death in 1791, the Methodist Conference expelled its most zealous members for holding camp meetings. It disallowed Wesley's famed field preaching and women leaders. Wesley's teaching on sanctification called 'the second blessing' was thought to be too emotional, and contrary to the spirit of Methodism. The charismatic phase of Methodism was now overtaken by institutionalism.

In 1811, William Clowes and Hugh Borne formed the Primitive Methodists with the view of giving Methodism its revivalist, radical edge once more. Where once Wesley and his followers had been attacked by mobs, Methodists were now considered respectable; the wealthy and educated were counted among its ranks and a professional, male clergy took their places in its hierarchy. However, the 'Prims' drew the poor, uneducated and less respectable members of society; women and even children found a voice leading their meetings and in preaching.

The new wine

The challenge for us is to be continually filled with the Holy Spirit and be flexible containers to expand with the fermenting process of the new wine from heaven, whether that's individually or corporately. Jesus talked about this in Matthew 9:17,

Neither do men pour new wine into old wineskins. If they do, the skins will burst, the wine will run out and the wineskins will be ruined. No, they pour new wine into new wineskins, and both are preserved.

Each move of God has needed a new wineskin when the new wine has met with the inflexibility of the old. Jeremiah 2:13 says, *'My people have committed two sins: they have forsaken me, the spring of living water, and have dug their own cisterns, broken cisterns that cannot hold water.'* A broken cistern is a religious container that cannot hold the blessings of the Holy Spirit. It is rather like the Pharisees who believed themselves to be upholders of truth, whilst in reality they were missing Jesus who was the Truth.

Breaking the pattern of history

It's a sad fact of history that new moves of God have frequently not been welcomed and have even been persecuted by the previous one. There is always more to uncover. Let's embrace everything that God is doing in the world today and remember that the Holy Spirit will blow where he pleases (John 3:8). No one group has the ultimate truth.

This can be illustrated by Windsor Castle. Like Britain itself, the castle is steeped in history but is still a modern, working community.

In 1992, a devastating fire lasting fifteen hours burnt down an area of the State Apartments. Today that part of the castle has been carefully restored, by modern craftsmen using both new and ancient techniques. The new wood used to restore the damaged rooms was cut by precision lasers, but also called on old skills. There was a joining of the old and new to recreate something of beauty.

Intercessors who recently visited the castle spoke of that which is of God coming through the fire and being cleansed. Things from the past can be re-interpreted by modern craftsmen, with the old and new not just co-existing but complimenting each other. *'The kingdom of heaven is like the owner of a house who brings out of his storeroom new treasures as well as old'* (Matthew 13:52).

Searching the source

God spoke a key scripture to me which resulted in my last book, *Searching the Source of the River – Forgotten Women of the British Pentecostal Revival 1907.*(6) It was Job 28:11, *'He searches the sources of the rivers and brings hidden things to light.'*

At the source of every river of God, at the beginning of every denomination, there are hidden things that need to be brought into the light. So under what circumstances did these denominations begin? Was there a founding father? What was the revealed new 'truth' that believers gathered round?

Not every move of God or revival movement resulted in a new denomination, so it may appear that there are glaring omissions as we look further at the sources, but we'll pick up on revival movements in Britain's history in the next chapter.

The Protestant Reformation

Until 1517 there was one church, the Roman Catholic Church, a powerful alliance of church and state.

The Reformation introduced the new wine of salvation by grace through faith and the priesthood of believers. But the old wineskins remained in the guise of Lutheranism, which became the new form of the established church in Europe where it spread rapidly.

John Knox (1505-1572) spearheaded Protestantism in Scotland in the form of the Presbyterian Church. In England the Church of England was born out of the personal desires and political expediency of Henry VIII, resulting in the Parliamentary Act of Supremacy in 1534 when he was pronounced head of the Church of England.

Prior to this the soil had been prepared in Britain by John Wycliffe's translation of the Bible from Latin to English in 1382. Psalm 119:130 says, *'The unfolding of your words gives light'* and once the word of God was in the people's hands, the potential to expose deception and uncover truth was unleashed.

Open the king's eyes

William Tyndale (1494–1536) picked up Wycliffe's mantle. His translation of the Bible from Hebrew and Greek to English was completed in 1525. Tyndale's aim was, 'A copy in the hands of every man, woman and child in England' so that 'even the poorest ploughboy could read it.' He died a martyr and his last words as the flames licked his body were, 'Lord, open the king's eyes.'(7)

Within four years, Henry VIII ordered an English Bible to be chained to every pulpit and England became a Protestant country by law. The next few decades were a stormy time as the country swayed between Protestantism and Catholicism according to the dictates of the monarchs. Then in the time of the Commonwealth (1649–1660), Oliver Cromwell instituted a radical Puritanism in the land.

Opting out of Christendom

To the average 16th and 17th century mind it was inconceivable not to consider yourself to be part of the established church. Church and state were one, and the domain over which it exercised control was called Christendom. Although no longer part of the Roman Catholic system, the Church of England church had the same hierarchical structure and power as its counterpart.

So when various Spirit-led individuals and groups wanted to gather together outside this structure, they were considered subversive heretics who needed to be put in their place. Many such groups met in homes with local leaders and faced unspeakable persecution, until the Toleration Act of 1690 brought freedom of religion in Britain – at least in principle.

The Baptists

As their name suggests, the Baptists are so called because of their belief in adult baptism by immersion of believers, even if that person has been christened as a child.

The English Baptists can be traced back to a group of Separatists in Lincolnshire led by a former Anglican minister of Puritan persuasion, John Smyth, and a layman, Thomas Helwys. Following persecution they fled to Amsterdam in 1609. It was there, on studying the New Testament in Greek, that Smyth came to the conclusion that baptism is only valid on personal confession of faith. He first baptised himself and then his congregation.

In 1612 they returned to London and the first Baptist Church in England was begun under Helwys' leadership. By 1660 the number of congregations had grown to 300. Other Baptist fellowships sprung up which faced constant persecution but still grew in numbers. The largest of them was the forerunner of the Metropolitan Tabernacle (Spurgeon's Tabernacle) in London by the early 19th century.

The Anabaptists

After the Reformation a radical group formed known as the Anabaptists (re-baptisers), who thought that the Reformation hadn't gone far enough. They rapidly spread all over the continent, a highly charismatic community who practised prophecy and other spiritual gifts.

If the Reformation restored the truth of the priesthood of all believers, then the Anabaptists restored the truth of the prophethood of all believers.

Historians are divided about the relationship between the English Baptists and the Anabaptists. However, since both were exiled in Holland and some Anabaptists found their way to East Anglia, it is highly probable that there was some interaction between them. Certainly, the Mayflower leader John Robinson had been influenced by them.

The Religious Society of Friends
Another early group to opt out of Christendom were the Religious Society of Friends, or Quakers, in the 1650s. However they would never have considered themselves a denomination. In their eyes they were just 'friends' in line with the scripture where Christ told his disciples, *'I have called you friends'* (John 15:15).

The Friends met informally with no leaders and waited quietly for the Holy Spirit to move them to speak. Fellow 'friends' would bear witness, since the same Spirit lived in each one. The word Quaker was a derogatory term used by their opponents, because they noted that they trembled or quaked in the presence of the Lord.

The inner light
Their founder, Leicestershire-born George Fox (1624-1691), was from a Presbyterian/Puritan home. His first encounter with God at the age of 11 'awakened him to spiritual reality' which he later referred to as 'the inner light.' Full of unanswered questions, he left home at 19 and travelled round the country to find someone who could help him with his relationship with God. Then in 1647 the answer came straight from heaven, 'There is one, even Christ Jesus who can speak to thy condition.'

This experience cemented foundational truths into his life which formed the basis for the Friends' distinctive theology. This was based on John 1:1-14, especially verse 9 where it says that Jesus is *'The true light that gives light to every man has come into the world.'*

Friends believe that there is something of the light of God in everyone. By telling them the good news of the Gospel, they will respond and the flickering flame will be illumined again, like a candle wick held to a flame (Proverbs 20:27). This theology led them to believe in the value and equality of all mankind, in a day when one's place was fixed in the fabric of society.

Christ in you

Another key verse for the Friends was Colossians 1:27, *'Christ in you, the hope of glory.'* Christ, not the church, was the teacher and the Spirit of God the only guide through life. Theirs was an experiential Christianity where Christ could be known personally.

This led Fox to realise that the church was people, not a building or institution and he called the church buildings of the day 'steeple houses.' All this got him and his followers into major conflict with the civil and religious authorities. The Quaker Act of 1662 was passed to make the Friends swear an oath of allegiance to the king, something they refused to do. Then the Conventicle Act of 1664 forbade 'conventicles,' religious gatherings of more than five people outside the governance of the Church of England.

The Friends were one of the largest Spirit-led revival movements in our history, which we will consider in the next chapter, but they were also one of the most persecuted groups. Their theology spurred them to invest their lives in social reform and mission, a legacy that continues to the present day.

However, social reform eventually took over from signs and wonders as the movement became institutionalised. Even towards the end of Fox's life, the movement began showing a degree of organisation with its headquarters at Swarthmore Hall, and Fox referring to himself as 'the elder brother' amongst the brothers.

The Methodists

John Wesley (1703-1791) is a name that has cropped up several times already, and for someone who never meant to start a denomination, let the facts speak. Ten years after his death, there were 825 Wesleyan chapels in Britain with 90,000 members (8) when the population was around 10 million. (9) Wesley and his friend George Whitefield sparked the first evangelical awakening in the mid-18th century. Since then, Methodism in various forms has swept the world.

Like the 'Quakers,' the name 'Methodist' was a slur based on observations of a group of young men at Oxford. They had formed the Holy Club, seeking by 'methodical good works' to make themselves acceptable to God. John Wesley was a key leader of this group. Later, in the same vein he went as a missionary to Georgia, lamenting, 'I went to America to convert the Indians but oh, who will convert me?'(10)

As a young child he had been rescued from a fire in the family rectory in Epworth, Lincolnshire and knew his life had a special purpose. Ordained as a Church of England clergyman, he was loyal to the established church all his life and would never even preach at the same time as church services.

Salvation by faith
Wesley's godly mother Susanna taught him well, but John Wesley was always searching for a relationship with God rather than just religion. His prayers were answered when in 1738 his heart was 'strangely warmed' and he knew the 'assurance of salvation by faith in Christ alone.'(11) The next year he was overcome by the power of the Holy Spirit (12) and a passion burned inside of him for others to know the same experience.

A gospel of grace
Let the words of Wesley capture what was in his heart: 'What religion do I preach? The religion of love; the law of kindness brought to light by the gospel...to make all who receive it enjoy God and themselves; to make them like God; lovers of all; contented in their lives; and crying out at their death, in calm assurance, 'O grave, where is thy victory?'(13)

The world his parish
Wesley's enthusiasm was not welcomed by the establishment, who believed that salvation was only to be found within the church, and opposed the doctrine of new birth. He was banned from preaching within the churches and so began years of travelling the length and breadth of Britain and Ireland preaching under market crosses, in the fields or wherever crowds would gather. He famously commented, 'The world is my parish.'(14)

Over a fifty-year period of ministry he covered 250,000 miles in the saddle,(15) preached 42,000 sermons and trained 192 travelling preachers.(16) He left 72,000 people in 87 Methodist societies around Britain and 27 in Ireland.(17)

In the quaint language of the day, he said that 'he submitted to be more vile' (18) as he took the gospel of salvation to the masses and the common people went to hear him in droves.

An organisational genius

I'll be looking at the birth, extent and fruit of the revival in later chapters, but Wesley's genius was in his organisational skills. He formed his converts into 'classes' for mutual encouragement, prayer and Bible study, and where there were several classes they became a 'society' with a trained lay overseer. They were interdenominational and the first was the Foundry Chapel in Fetter Lane, London, in 1739. The towns of London, Bristol and Newcastle formed a triangle of the main centres of Methodism in Britain. He made disciples, not just converts.

Entire sanctification

During his life, Wesley had chosen as his successor, the theologian Revd. John Fletcher. Unfortunately Fletcher died first, but not before his notion of Christian Perfection, or Entire Sanctification, entered into Wesley's preaching as a second blessing experience. This formed the basis of the 19th century holiness teaching, and subsequent baptism of the Holy Spirit terminology of the Pentecostals.

Lacking any obvious successor with the charisma and stature of John Wesley, a Methodist Conference took over the leadership of the movement and its 'charismatic moment' began to pass. As we have seen, in a reaction to the creeping institutionalism, the Primitive Methodists emerged in 1811.

The Brethren

As another reaction to formal, hierarchical Christianity, the Brethren were formed in 1828. They attracted those who were looking for simplicity of worship, like the Quakers before them. Many joined them from the Church of England and their numbers increased as they upheld the truth of the priesthood of believers.

George Muller is well known for his orphanage of 2000 children in Bristol which he supported by faith alone. He became the leader of the Open Brethren as they parted company from J.N. Derby who formed the Exclusive Brethren in 1848.

Derby gained fame with his pre-millennial dispensationalist teaching immortalised by the Scofield Reference Bible. Unlike the exclusives, as their name suggests, the Open Brethren sought fellowship with Christians of other denominations. Both have always had a strong emphasis on Bible teaching and mission, and gained many converts from the 1859 revival.

The Salvation Army

The Salvation Army, founded by William and Catherine Booth, emerged from the mid-19th century evangelical awakening and revival of holiness. William Booth became the pastor of a Methodist chapel in Gateshead in the North East of England in 1858 where Wesley had had major success. A fiery evangelist and preacher, Booth had been converted under the influence of American revivalist James Caughey and revival fire had entered his bones. His chapel soon became dubbed the 'Converting Shop' as 2000 packed the daily meetings that continued for four months.

The couple also came under the influence of American revivalists, Walter and Phoebe Palmer, whose successful four-year ministry tour of Britain (1859-63) greatly impacted the North East. Preacher Phoebe was a role model for the young Catherine, and after a powerful encounter with the Lord at Pentecost 1860, Catherine announced that she had wronged the Lord by refusing to speak; that night she preached to a packed house. Together the Booths became one of the most well-known husband-and-wife ministry teams in Britain to this day.

Send the Fire

As well as the evangelistic thrust of their ministry, preaching the power of the blood of Christ, they believed that the fire of God could so come on a believer that they could be 'made holy' as a second blessing experience.

Clues to this are found in Booth's powerful hymn, (19) 'O God of burning, cleansing flame, send the fire' where that power enabled a believer 'to walk the world in white,' in purity before God and the world. The Salvation Army was part of the Holiness movement of the 19th century which embraced this theology.

A Plan to Bless the World

The Booths carried revival to Cornwall in 1861-2 and thousands were converted wherever they went. Booth formed 'Hallelujah Bands', new converts with colourful backgrounds who carried the gospel to those like them. One band consisted of a prize fighter, a pickpocket, a convicted train robber and a bear baiter! It sounds like David's mighty men (1 Samuel 22:2).

Whilst staying at a friend's house in Walsall in the English Midlands, William was asked by his host what he was doing pacing up and down the garden. The answer, 'My friend, I am thinking out a plan which, when it is implemented, will mean blessing to the wide, wide, world'!(20) Prophetic words indeed.

Blood and Fire

Whilst welcoming the revival, the Methodist conference was stirred to jealousy by their itinerant ministry, and Catherine's prominence was not approved of in some quarters. So it was that after seeing the appalling need in the East End of London, the joint expression of evangelism and social transformation gave birth to the Salvation Army in 1875. In true militaristic style they wore a uniform and marched under the banner of 'Blood and Fire,' waging war on the evils of society and snatching sinners from the clutches of Satan.

The Pentecostals

Like the Methodists before them, Pentecostalism in Britain was born in the Church of England and its leader was the Revd. Alexander Alfred Boddy who, like John Wesley, had no intention of starting another denomination. Early Pentecostalism's co-leader was the aristocratic Anglican, Cecil Polhill.

By the turn of the 20th century the word 'Pentecostal' had come to describe those in any denomination who were looking for an experience subsequent to conversion, a second blessing not just for holiness but for power. Following the Azusa Street outpouring in April 1906 in Los Angeles where people began to speak in tongues as they were baptised in the Holy Spirit (Acts 2:2-4), hunger for this 'sign' of Spirit baptism grew amongst believers in Britain.

Boddy, who was the vicar of All Saints' Church, Monkwearmouth, Sunderland, on the north east coast of England and his wife, Mary, were among that company.

Tongues and healing

The Holy Spirit descended in a series of special meetings from 1st September 1907. All Saints' became a well for the revival in Britain attracting Christians from far and near who were seeking the baptism of the Holy Spirit. The gift of speaking in tongues and healing were the two distinctive features of the movement.

There were highly influential, annual conferences called the Sunderland Conventions which continued till 1914 and *Confidence*, a monthly magazine, both of which disseminated the Pentecostal message and carried it worldwide. The early Pentecostals believed that they were experiencing an outpouring of 'the latter rain' to gather a worldwide harvest. In their view, tongues had been given to bypass language learning, so there was a huge missionary emphasis in the movement.

The Assemblies and Elim

After the First World War (1914-18) Boddy, who had supported the war, was at odds with many Pentecostals who had been pacifists and some of the original fire was lost. A new leadership was emerging who wanted autonomy. So it was that in 1923 the Pentecostal denomination of the Assemblies of God was started, which followed the founding of the Elim denomination in 1915.

A 1935 commentary (21) regarding the Pentecostals explains the now-familiar story, 'In consequence of the [Anglican] Church's official attitude, which was Pharisaical, numbers of Christians found themselves virtually excommunicated, and generally met together in back street mission halls and in private houses. The result was that Pentecost went back to the upper room and stayed there, except for a few urgent souls who became foreign missionaries.'

Pentecostals have now long emerged from the upper room and with their charismatic brothers and sisters from all denominations have found a new unity in the Spirit. How things have changed!

Back to the vision

The founding fathers of these denominations had life in their bones and they faithfully stewarded the vision that God gave them in their day and generation. But the revelation was meant to be kept alive like the fire that the Levites were to keep burning on the altar (Leviticus 6:12). It was to never go out.

I am reminded of Ezekiel's valley of dry bones (Ezekiel 37). They needed a prophetic voice to breathe life into them, so they could rise again as a vast army.

I believe it is possible for an organisation to have life breathed back into it so it becomes a living organism. I feel a challenge for existing denominations to discover the original fire as many have, honour their spiritual fathers and mothers, tell the family stories, let the life of past revivals enter their soul and allow their spirits to be quickened.

Denominations tell the story of God's involvement in human history worked out through relationships with groups or individuals, whereas denominationalism only speaks of quenched fire. There is a difference.

I want it all!

Thinking about the distinctive of these denominations, the truths they gathered round were precious and still are. I want to be among a people who embrace them all! I cherish the truths of the reformers who sought to live in right relationship with God through faith and grace alone, with no performance necessary.

Like all the post-reformation sects, such as the Baptists, I want to find warmth and fellowship among believers and be unafraid to take a stand for revealed truth. I want to be like the Friends, who valued the gold in all humanity and sought to be led by the Spirit. I want to experience 'religion of the heart' like Wesley, where love and grace trump judgement.

I also want to live on the radical edge like the 'Prims' and, moreover, to have the understanding of the Brethren who understood that we are all priests before God. I want, like the Salvation Army, to love purity, and war against sin wherever it is found. I want to experience the power of the Holy Spirit like the Pentecostals, and value all the gifts of the Spirit, including tongues.

And I believe there is *still* more truth and light yet to break forth from God's holy word!

Endnotes

1. www.wikipedia.org/wiki/John_Robinson_(pastor)

2. Ibid.

3. *Confidence*, October 1913, p 196.

4. A. Skevington Wood, *The Burning Heart*, Cliff College Publishing, Sheffield, 2001, p 199.

5. Susan Hyatt, *In the Spirit We're Equal*, Hyatt Press, Dallas, USA, 1998, p 140.

6. Diana Chapman, *Searching the Source of the River – Forgotten Women of the Pentecostal Revival in Britain*, Push Publishing, London, 2007.

7. www.ccel/f/foxe/martyrs/home.html Ed. William Byron Forbush, *Fox's Book of Martyrs* (online) Chapter XII *The Life and Story of the True Servant and Martyr of God, William Tyndale*, originally published 1563.

8. John Pollock, *Wesley the Preacher*, Kingsway Publications, Eastbourne, UK, 2000, book description.

9. The 1801 census estimated the population of England and Wales to be 8.9 million, Scotland 1.6 million. Ireland was not included in the census until 1821.

10. Skevington Wood, op.cit., p 57.

11. See Chapter 1, endnote xii.

12. See Chapter 5.

13. Skevington Wood, op.cit., pp 147-8.

14. Skevington Wood, op.cit., p 106.

15. J. Edwin Orr, *The Second Evangelical Awakening in Britain*, Marshall, Morgan and Scott, London, Edinburgh, UK, 1949, p 264.

16. Pollock, op.cit., book description.

17. Minutes of the Methodist Conference, 1791.

18. Skevington Wood, op.cit., p 92.

19. William Booth, *Send the Fire*, 1894.

20. Orr, op.cit., p 139.

21. Patrick Dixon, *Signs of Revival*, Kingsway Publications, Eastbourne, U.K., 1994, p 181, quoting James McWhirter in the foreword of *Pentecostal Rays, a Pentecostal History* by George Jeffries, 1935.

4
Deposits of Gold

*Oh, that you would rend the heavens and come down, that the
mountains would tremble before you... you did awesome things that
we did not expect, you came down.* Isaiah 64:1, 3

Times of refreshing
There have been times in our history when God has rent the heavens
and come down. Peter, standing before the crowd fresh from the upper
room, described them as, 'times of refreshing from the presence of the
Lord' (Acts 4:19). Call them what you will, times of visitation, kairos
moments, revivals, awakenings...

They are times when there is an invasion of heavenly realities into the
earth realm. Isn't that what Jesus told us to pray for? 'Your kingdom come,
let your will be done on earth as it is in heaven' (Matthew 6:10).

Truly I believe that as individuals we are meant to live every day of our
lives as if heaven were near. However, this chapter is devoted to moments
in Britain's history when the gold of heaven has been deposited in the
strata of time.

Revival waves
I like the following definition of revivals and awakenings: 'Revival is
the revitalizing of a body of Christian believers, and awakening is the
stirring of interest in the Christian faith among nominal Christians or
unbelievers.'(1)

There have been a series of revivals in Britain since we emerged from the Dark Ages. Some have been national, awakening the whole country to spiritual realities and causing great social change. Others have been local but still had a remarkable impact on the areas involved. And then there are all shades in between!

Let this, written in the last century, send shivers down your spine...

It is by revivals of religion that the church of God makes its most visible advance. When all things seem becalmed, when no breath stirs the air, when the sea is like lead and the sky is low and gray, when all worship seems to have ended but the worship of matter, then it is that the Spirit of God is poured upon the church, then it is that the Christianity of the apostles and martyrs, not that of the philosophers and liberals, keeps rising...from the catacombs of oblivion, and appears young and fresh in the midst of the obsolete things of yesterday and the day before.(2)

Spirit-led movements

The waves of revivals we will be looking at in this chapter begin as the power of God's word in the English language touched the hearts and minds of the common people, causing them to hunger for New Testament Christianity. They were Spirit-led movements and those who allowed themselves to be swept along ran the risk of severe persecution.

The established church authorities used the marriage of Church and State as a means of controlling the general population. A heretic was someone who didn't toe the line, possibly just a Christian who wanted to follow the Holy Spirit rather than man's laws. It wasn't until 1689 that nonconformity was at least tolerated, when an act of parliament paved the way for religious freedom.

As we saw in the last chapter, some of these revivals developed into new denominations, but not all did. Some were pan-denominational; there were also forces of renewal within established denominations and the Church of England itself.

From the 14th to the 20th century, almost every century has seen a Spirit-led revival, some more.

- **14th century** – The Lollards
- **16th and 17th centuries** – Puritans and Quakers

- **18th century** – the first evangelical awakening was catalysed by the preaching of George Whitefield and John Wesley. It resulted in the establishment of Methodism and the beginning of social change and missionary endeavour.
- **19th century** – the second evangelical awakening began in 1859, affecting all denominations including the Church of England and spawning new gatherings in chapels across the country. Social reforms and an explosion of mission work followed in its wake (see Chapter 8). There was a popular revival of holiness. By the turn of the century there was a heightened expectation in Britain for a great move of God, which was not disappointed!
- **20th century** – nationally, the 1904-5 Welsh revival and the 1907-14 Pentecostal revival, and locally, the 1949-52 Hebrides and 1921 East Anglia revivals

Morning stars

Revivals which include a revelation of newly discovered truths or spiritual experiences often are led by men or women who have lived ahead of their time. They are forerunners, who see things and act before the general Christian populace. Often shunned by the majority and emerging from the margins, they usher in a new move of the Spirit and 'pull into their day what is reserved for another day.'(3)

These men and women of vision and courage point the direction in which the Spirit of God is moving, just as John the Baptist was a voice in the desert pointing to Jesus (John 1:23). Sometimes called 'morning stars,' they light the way at the dawn of a new day for the church.

One such man was Edward Irving, 'the Morning Star of Pentecostalism' under whose ministry in London in 1820s and 30s there was speaking in tongues and exercise of the gifts of the Spirit, some 70 years before the Pentecostal revival.

14th century street evangelists

Another earlier example was Oxford scholar, John Wycliffe (1329-1384), known as 'The Morning Star of the Reformation.' He sent out his 'apostolic men,' an order of 'poor priests,' the length and breadth of Britain. They carried tracts, sermons and the Bible, all in the newly translated English language, and preached about Jesus wherever they could find an audience.

These 14th century street evangelists lived and dressed simply, and found sympathy among the common people. However, unsurprisingly they were vehemently opposed by the church authorities, who dubbed Wycliffe's followers 'Lollards,' which means 'babblers.'

One contemporary of Wycliffe claimed, 'They were everywhere. A man could scarcely meet two people on the road but one of them was a disciple of Wycliffe.'(4) Even if this is an exaggeration it shows their hugely significant influence on the British people at that time.

If this were to happen today, we would no doubt call it a 'revival.' However, it was a risky business being a Lollard. Some faced martyrdom, and Wycliffe himself was excommunicated.

In their line today, stand the Wycliffe Bible Translators who at this present time are working in ninety-nine countries to give them the word of God in their own languages.

A desire for purity

To be called 'puritanical' is now synonymous with being a legalistic killjoy, something most Christians today would want to distance themselves from. However following the English Protestant reformation of 1534, the Puritans, as their name suggests, were those within the ranks of the Church of England who desired a simpler or purer form of biblical Christianity. After the 1662 Act of Uniformity they began to leave the established church and set up independent congregations.

Like all revivals in its early days, this was a true move of the Spirit. Puritans stood for freedom and toleration, breathing life into dead religion. They gave us John Bunyan, who spent twelve years in prison for preaching without a licence, where he wrote The Pilgrim's Progress, said to be the second-most translated book next to the Bible. Theologian Richard Baxter's preaching ministry drew large crowds and it is said that his study walls were stained with his praying breath. (5)

The Puritans kept the light of gospel burning in the 16th and 17th century, and from them emerged the Baptists, Congregationalists and Quakers. Many went into exile in Holland or sailed to find freedom in the New World.

The Quaker revival

Out of all the revival movements in our history, I consider the Friends' revival of the 17th century the most remarkable. They achieved amazing things when the odds were so stacked against them. Persecution and imprisonment was an everyday occurrence.

At one time there were 15,000 Friends in prison and they faced public hangings. Fox, their leader, was imprisoned over 100 times. Women were whipped and beaten and their children sold into slavery, yet within a generation they were the fastest growing movement in the Western world, numbering 60,000 by 1600 (6) when the population was around 5 million. (7)

By the turn of the 17th century, ten percent of the English population was Quaker. Even some established churches had been emptied of members. Nothing less than a supernatural grace and enabling rested upon them, and they certainly challenge our cosy 21st century existence.

A man becomes a movement

It's one thing for a man to be transformed by the Holy Spirit; it's another for that man to become a movement. Early in his ministry, Fox had a vision when he was on top of Pendle Hill in Lancashire. He saw a sea covering the land and the Lord showed him where the people would be responsive to his preaching. True to his vision, he went to these places and preached all over Britain, Holland and even America.

All sorts of people flocked to hear him preach and became 'convinced' by his message. Itinerant preachers called 'the Valiant 60' emerged from the ranks and carried revival fire up and down the country and over the seas. These men and women represented all classes of society and preached in taverns, prisons, universities and gatherings in homes as they were led by the Spirit.

A book of miracles

For the first time in the history of Britain there was a national Spirit-led revival movement where supernatural and spiritual gifts were the norm. Signs did indeed follow the preaching of the word (see Chapter 6) and their good fruit remained, securing many of the freedoms we enjoy today, but that's for Chapter 8.

The first Evangelical awakening – the 18th century

In the early 1700s, Britain was in a sorry state of moral decay. Outside the public houses there were signs announcing, 'Drunk for a penny, dead drunk for two pence. Straw to lie on.'(8) Generally the churches were unconcerned. It took two clerics who were also old friends to shake the nation and awaken it to spiritual realities. They were George Whitefield and John Wesley, who had been part of the Holy Club whilst at Oxford University.

Whitefield, born in a tavern in Gloucester, had his own personal awakening in 1735. He began preaching the gospel of salvation at the age of 22 and literally thousands came to hear him. He once said, 'God enabled me to preach with the demonstration of the Spirit and with power so that I could lift up my voice like a trumpet.'(9) All before PA systems!

Over 34 years Whitefield preached over 30,000 times in his unique, theatrical style. He went to America seven times where he was instrumental along with Jonathan Edwards in America's first Great Awakening in the 18th century.

Field preaching

Whitefield pioneered open-air preaching first to the rough coal miners in Kingswood, Bristol, where within two weeks the crowds reached 20,000. He then went on to London where crowds of up to 60,000 stood out on the commons in all weathers to hear him. On one Sunday 80,000 people gathered at Mayfair, near Hyde Park and Whitefield commented, 'I have indeed seen the kingdom of God come with power in this great city.' Referring to his time in Bristol he wrote, 'Oh that such a fire may not be kindled but blow up all England into a flame, and all the world over.'(10) Whitefield travelled the length and breadth of Britain with startling results. He worked with Howell Harris who was bringing revival to Wales, and sparked a revival in Cambuslang, Scotland in 1742 when up to 30,000 gathered to hear him preach. At one time there followed weeping and repentance that continued for one and a half hours. It was Whitefield who first introduced Wesley to field preaching and as he spent more and more time in America, Wesley became the British face of the Awakening.

The Moravian connection

The spirit of revival is catching. John Wesley was greatly influenced by contact with some Moravians who were part of the revival movement in Herrnhut, Germany led by Count Nicholas von Zinzendorf. They had a 'rent-heaven' experience in one of their meetings in 1727 when it's said that they didn't know whether they were in heaven or on earth. They sent out hundreds of missionaries and became famous for their prayer meeting that lasted a hundred years.

Wesley's first encounter with the Moravians was in a storm on his way to America. He was afraid, but the Moravians sung hymns and had a peace he knew he didn't possess. When back in England he sought out the Moravian community, looking for spiritual reality.

Moravian Peter Boehler advised Wesley to preach faith in Jesus until the feelings came. Amazingly, people were finding peace with God even though Wesley didn't possess it himself, that is until the day when his heart was 'strangely warmed.'(11) Following this experience, Wesley visited Herrnhut to catch more of their fire.

The revival really began in 1737 after a powerful encounter with God at a New Year's Eve prayer meeting in London (see Chapter 5). The revival initially appealed to the poor and marginalised of society, such as the Bristol miners. The churches didn't want these rough and ready converts, and so Wesley began societies and trained lay men and women to lead them.

Consumed by his message

Wesley was totally consumed with preaching the message of justification by faith through grace alone. He continued to his death in 1791 aged 87, one of the concessions to his age being a change in transport from the saddle to a carriage. During his lifetime he travelled a quarter of a million miles, preached 42,000 sermons and found time to write over 200 books.(12) He left 72,000 Methodists but many more had been influenced by his message.(13) What a legacy!

He was an itinerant who evangelised Britain in the same manner as Aidan and Cuthbert's men and Augustine's monks, Wycliffe's Lollards and Fox's 'Valiant Sixty.' In the open air they reached the masses who would have never considered entering a church building. It was evangelism in the context of revival and the Spirit of God was moving everywhere. Wesley came unannounced and on occasions tens of thousands gathered to hear him preach. Crowds even gathered at five in the morning.

Wesley's method was, figuratively speaking, to set himself ablaze and let men come and see him burn!

He famously said, 'Give me a hundred men, I care not a straw whether they be clergymen or laymen, such alone will shake the gates of hell and set up the kingdom of God on earth.'(14)

While on his way to change the world, his message changed the face of Britain. It may have not happened immediately, but as lives were revolutionised, the yeast of the gospel did its work to propel men and women into good works that began the transformation of society (see Chapter 8).

Journaling

We should be very grateful to Wesley that in 'methodical' fashion he kept a journal that is available today. It charts the good, the bad and the ugly of his ministry and gives us an insight into the man, his methods and beliefs.

It wasn't all glowing success and he faced angry mobs in many places. Like many revivalists his preaching was accompanied by emotional scenes, some wild in the extreme and supernatural occurrences such as healings and deliverances. These 'signs' even made Wesley and Whitefield wonder (see Chapter 6)!

The extent and depth of revival

In 1777, Wesley's new chapel in the City of London was opened (the same one we visited in Chapter 1). At the accompanying ceremony he reviewed the work so far.

This revival of religion has spread to such a degree, as neither we nor our fathers had known. How extensive has it been! There is scarce a considerable town in the kingdom, where some have not been made witness of it. It has spread to every age and sex, to most orders and degrees of men; and even in abundance of those who, in time past, were accounted monsters of wickedness...

We may likewise observe the depth of the work so extensively and swiftly wrought. Multitudes have been thoroughly convinced of sin; and, shortly after, so filled with joy and love, that whether they were in the body, or out of the body, they could hardly tell; and, in the power of this love, they have trampled underfoot whatever the world accounts either terrible or desirable, having evidenced, in the severest trials, an invariable and tender goodwill to mankind, and all the fruits of holiness.(15)

Theology in song

John's brother, Charles was a prolific hymn writer and put Wesley's theology into song. He often used popular tunes of the day, with words which today powerfully carry the heart of the revival into the 21st century.

So near the throne

Unfortunately as the revival progressed, a difference of opinion developed between Wesley and Whitefield. By conviction Wesley held Arminian views, whereas Whitefield was a Calvinist. Wesley alone also believed that 'entire sanctification' was possible and preached holiness.

The story goes that one day someone asked Whitefield if he would see Wesley in heaven. He replied, 'No,' but explained that Wesley would be so near to the throne of God he wouldn't be able to see him. Such humility and grace won the day, and oiled the machinery of the revival as it swept Britain for 50 years.

Camp Meeting Methodists

As this revival wave receded, it left deposits on the soil of this land. Methodism had been established, the good fruit remained and grew, but it needed the spiritual momentum of the Primitive Methodists to capture the revivalism of Wesley's day.

Influenced by American-style camp meetings, Hugh Borne and William Clowes organised the first English camp meeting at Mow Cop, the highest point on the Pennine Mountains in the north of England. It was May 1807, people came from miles around and it was a great success.

Oh dear, the Methodist Conference disapproved. It said that camp meetings were 'allowable in America but highly improper in England'! (16) Expelled from main-stream Methodism, the Camp Meeting Methodists became the Primitive Methodists in 1811.

These popular open-air camp meetings continued all over Britain with attendances of 10–20,000. They were accompanied by scenes of revival power as the Holy Spirit was poured out on the gatherings. They built several thousand chapels like the one in the street where I live and by the end of the 19th century, the number of 'Prims' in Britain reached 212,000. To mark the centennial of Mow Cop, 100,000 people assembled once again for one big spiritual jamboree!(17)

Revivalism kept alive

In the years between the two awakenings, as well as the Prims, an Irish-American Methodist preacher called James Caughey kept the fires burning. He believed that God was calling him to visit Britain, but he didn't go until he knew he had received the anointing he required. He spent several days seeking God, praying on his face in a field near Baltimore, until the fire of the Holy Spirit fell on him and he leapt to his feet crying, 'I can go now!'

He got the timing right and during the six years he spent here in the 1840s, he saw over 20,000 saved, including the young William Booth. They called him 'the king of revivalist preachers,' and Caughey returned to Britain again in 1857 and twice in the 1860s. Although a Methodist, he was far too unrespectable for the Methodist establishment and his methods were frowned upon. It certainly didn't deter him, or the people that poured out to hear him.

The second Evangelical awakening – the 19th century

In 1860 the 'Prince of Preachers,' C.H. Spurgeon wrote, 'The times of refreshing from the presence of the Lord have at last dawned upon our land. A spirit of prayer is visiting our churches. The first breath of the rushing mighty wind is already discerned, while on rising evangelists the tongues of fire have evidently descended.'(18)

Revival had broken out in America and all over Northern Ireland spontaneously in 1857-8. The whole of Scotland first felt the fire in 1858 and every county in Wales and England was affected by 1859-60. Although God raised up amazingly gifted men and women to carry the flames, this revival didn't have a Whitefield, Wesley or Fox or even an Evan Roberts, and probably for that reason it is less well known.

There were of course William and Catherine Booth, but the names of Henry Grattan Guinness, Brownlow North, David Morgan, Reginald Radcliffe, Richard Weaver, Hay Aitkin (the list goes on!) don't readily spring to the mind of the average Christian. Perhaps they should.

Staggered by the statistics

I have been blown away by the sheer numbers involved.(19) The converts in Northern Ireland and other parts of Ireland exceeded 100,000. The figure for Wales was 100,000; Scotland gained 300,000 and England around 800,000. So a conservative estimate of 1 million over 5 years for the whole United Kingdom would mean a staggering 27% of the population were Christians, the population being 27 million at the time.

The churches worked together, and all denominations benefited. Many embarked on church building programmes, including the Church of England. Although the crest of the revival wave lasted around five years, the wash affected Britain for the next fifty years. Just contrast this short period with the lifetime results of Wesley and Whitefield's preaching, and it gives an idea of the impact of the revival.

It must be understood that this revival was not just about numbers of converts, but radically changed lives and communities. This is what happens when heaven comes down; a nation can be changed. This mid-19th century awakening brought Christian values yet again to Britain.

It resulted not just in evangelism and mission, but in a social conscience that was to transform society as in the wake of Methodism, which we will read about in Chapter 8. It also created hunger for a deepening of the spiritual life with a revival of Holiness.

A prayer meeting in Northern Ireland

The revival in Northern Ireland began in May 1857. It was the same month as the prayer meeting in New York which sparked the Second Great Awakening in America with one million converts in the first two years. (20)

Having been challenged by the story of George Muller's faith, new convert James McQuilkin and three friends met in a schoolhouse in Kells, County Antrim, every Friday evening to pray. Just as in the States, people were moved by the Holy Spirit and the prayer meetings multiplied.

A special meeting was held in Ahoghill in 1859. So many attended that it was too dangerous to stay in the building, and 3,000 fell to their knees and faces in the muddy streets outside as they listened to the preacher. From that, the revival spread to north and south alike and made a greater spiritual impact on Ireland than the days of Saint Patrick. (21)

Heaven comes to Scotland

The awakening in Scotland began in Aberdeen and swept the Lowlands,

Highlands and Islands. News from America and Northern Ireland had provoked similar prayer meetings and thousands flocked into the churches for meetings that lasted for hours. 'Whole congregations [were] bending before it like in a rushing mighty wind.' Reports told of countless changed lives, and one person summed up the general feeling when they said that they never expected to see so much of heaven this side of time.

The spirit of praise in Wales

A son of Wales, Humphrey Jones returned to his homeland carrying revival from the States which he had caught from preacher David Morgan. Prayer and revival meetings sprang up all over the principality, some with 30,000 in the congregation, one lasting 18 hours. They were characterised by praise and singing. Preaching was taken to the pubs and prayer meetings were held in the mines. All Wales was shaken.

Theatre services in London

By January 1860 in London there were 200 prayer meetings, some daily, some weekly. Many West End theatres such as the famous Sadler's Wells and the Garrick opened their doors for Sunday evening services where 50,000 unchurched entered each week and hundreds were turned away.(22) Opponents called them 'religious pantomimes.'

Lord Shaftsbury campaigned to legalise church services in unconsecrated buildings, writing, 'Any church that is...unsuitable to the poor, disliked by the poor, and deserted by the poor, has failed in the same degree in one main object of its establishment.'(23) London had a revival of preaching with such success that spiritual births outstripped the natural birth rate.

All Britain is reached

Preaching evangelists travelled round the country and revival in cities, towns and villages followed them. Prayer meetings were full to overflowing and major universities such as Oxford and Cambridge profoundly impacted. There were gentlemen preachers who reached their own class, as well as the likes of William Booth's 'Hallelujah Bands,' made up of former drunkards and reformed criminals who were also highly effective in reaching their own.

Transatlantic revivalism

During this period, more fuel was added to revival fire in Britain by visits of revivalists from the States. Caughey returned, and Charles Finney who had visited twice in the 1840 came again in 1859-60, bringing revival to several of our large cities. Revivalist D.L. Moody, himself a product of the Awakening, began his evangelistic career in York in 1873, the first of many successful visits.

A revival of holiness

Like the Booths, American husband-and-wife team Walter and Phoebe Palmer carried revival. They toured major cities and towns of Britain from 1959-63 with amazing success. Fresh from the revival in Hamilton, Canada, they taught holiness.

This revival of holiness had arrived in Britain from the States from the Methodist camp and fuelled the desire for something 'more,' building on Wesley's doctrine of entire sanctification as a second blessing. Called the 'deeper' or 'higher Christian life,' it had increasingly gained popularity and found expression as an emotional experience subsequent to conversion. It was explained as being the baptism of the Holy Spirit.

Although Phoebe's meetings were emotionally charged, she had developed her own take on holiness. (24) She called Christians to lay their lives on the altar and claim sanctification by faith, which she called 'naked faith in the naked word.' Wherever the Palmers went, thousands came to hear her.

The saving presence of Christ

Phoebe writes of the time in Sunderland in October 1859 in her book, Four Years in the Old World. (25) 'The work here bids fair to exceed anything we remember to have witnessed either in America or Europe.' Three thousand a night were coming to her meetings there, and many were turned away. People were 'saved by the score daily' and there were many healings.

One night the chapel door had to be locked one and a half hours before the meeting started so no more people could try and squeeze themselves in! Meetings ended at ten o'clock 'but hundreds lingered, unwilling to leave the place so hallowed by the saving presence of Christ.'

Interdenominational holiness groups sprang up all over Britain in the second half of the 19th century, using Pentecostal language. They were held in a loose association called the Pentecostal League.

Keswick Conventions

If the revivalism and holiness of the mid-19th century awakening could be institutionalised, then it was in the annual Keswick Conventions which began in 1875 in the English Lake District and which continue to this day. Holiness teachers from both sides of the Atlantic were the speakers and the hungry from all denominations flocked to hear them. It was the place to go.

Instrumental in Keswick's formation were another holiness husband-and-wife team from the States, Hannah and Robert Whitall Smith. Keswick 'holiness' was taught as a more progressive experience than Phoebe's, but by the end of the century, whatever camp you were from, 'the baptism in the Holy Spirit' and 'spiritual gifts' had entered Christian vocabulary.

Millennial expectation was high and Britain was poised for a new wave of revival. Just prior to the Welsh revival, American revivalist R.A. Torrey had further saturated our land.

The 1904 Welsh revival

Never underestimate the power of a simple testimony. In February 1904 at a youth meeting in Newquay, South Wales, 15-year-old Florrie Evans, a convert of only three weeks stood to testify in her native Welsh, 'I do love the Lord Jesus with all my heart.'(26)

The minister, Joseph Jenkins wrote that, 'An unaccountable power accompanied her simple testimony and seemed to overwhelm the people...the meetings multiplied...people everywhere [were] electrified by...intense passion.' He continued, 'The Spirit of God has fallen on our young people. I am unable to do anything. I am in the middle of the sound of a wind. God himself is here. I have never seen anything like it.'(27) He sent them to chapels all over South Wales carrying revival fire.

Bend me

One of these chapels was in Blaenannerch. Hungry for more of God, 26-year-old Evan Roberts, who was training for the ministry in nearby

Newcastle Emlyn, attended a meeting on September 24th 1904. He looked back on this day as the beginning of what became known as the Welsh revival when 70,000 were swept into the kingdom in the first two months, more than 100,000 in five months, and still more during the eighteen months it lasted. Its impact reverberated round the rest of Britain and many parts of the world.

Evan wrote about that meeting in his diary, 'I fell on my knees with my arms on the seat in front of me and the tears and perspiration flowed freely...I cried, "Bend me, bend me, bend me, bend us"...O wonderful grace...What bent me was God commending his love and I not seeing anything in it to commend...After I was bent a wave of peace came over me, O wonderful love. This is life.'(28)

God took hold of Evan

From that day the Spirit of God took hold of Evan and he told his friend Sidney Evans, 'I've got wonderful news for you. I had a vision of all Wales being lifted up to heaven. We are going to see the mightiest revival that Wales has ever known – and the Holy Spirit is coming just now. We must get ready. We must have a little band and go all over the country preaching.'(29)

Praying multitudes

He began in his home church, Moriah Chapel, Loughor, and the momentum gathered. Regular prayer meetings continued till three in the morning and the chapel overflowed as Evan, always seeking to be led by the Spirit, preached and prayed his way through the night. Newspapers carried the stories (see Chapter 1 and endnote 6) and the crowds flocked to the little chapel. As one minister remarked, 'The community has been converted into a praying multitude.'(30)

Evan travelled the valleys with a group of young revivalists, many of whom were women, and there were the same scenes wherever they went. It was a revival of emotional faith.

One eyewitness reported, 'Such marvellous singing, quite extempore, could only have been created by a supernatural power – the Holy Spirit. No choir, no conductor, no organ – just spontaneous, unctionised soul singing. Once the first hymn was given out, the meeting conducted itself. There was no leader, but people felt an unseen control. Singing, sobbing, praying intermingled and proceeded without intermission.'(31) There was confession of sin, as well as testimonies, visions, prophesies and teaching on the end times. Such were the hallmarks of the revival. Often Evan's presence was incidental.

The love song of the Welsh revival

One song in particular was sung by Annie Davies and it became the anthem for the revival: 'Here is love, vast as the ocean.' Wherever she sung it, people would break down and weep. We still sing it today and its haunting melody and words convey the love affair God has with his people as he 'kisses a guilty world in love.'(32)

The revival spread

The revival first affected the grass-root mining communities and then spread all over Wales. Its social impact was profound and a holy presence lingered over the principality. It was a true awakening in every sense of the word.

Visitors came to observe what God was doing. One of these was Joseph Smaile who returned to Pasadena and helped pray in the Azusa Street Pentecostal revival of 1906. Even Welsh men and women as far away as Chile and India experienced revival. Its impact was truly worldwide.

It created a sense of expectancy and inspired prayer and belief that it could happen anywhere. It affected all denominations. The Society of Friends called it, 'Quakerism rebaptised.'(33) The 'children of the revival,' those who were converted during those years, included revivalists Stephen and George Jeffries who were to take Britain by storm in the 1920s and 30s.

The rest of Britain impacted

The heyday of the Welsh revival lasted 18 months. Worn out and misunderstood, Evan sadly withdrew from public ministry to rest; that story has been told elsewhere. But it's little realised how the awakening continued to impact the rest of Britain during the year 1905.

In town after town, revival swept the churches of all denominations, adding hundreds to their ranks. It happened spontaneously, and as in Wales, spilled out of the churches to affect entire communities. In places it was the topic of general conversation. Special trains were run to prayer meetings, theatres were used for evangelistic meetings once again and the Keswick Convention became a revival meeting. This phase of the revival was promoted by thirty Anglican bishops who recognised the season they were in.(34)

A world swept by the Spirit

Early in 1904, Roberts had said prophetically, 'I believe the world is upon the threshold of a great religious revival...the world will be swept by his Spirit as by a rushing mighty wind.'(35) Partly fulfilled by the Welsh revival, this is exactly what happened as the Holy Spirit was poured out in the Pentecostal revival.

The Pentecostal revival 1907

Rather than look at the national impact of the 20th century Pentecostal revival in Britain, I think it is more important to see it as part of a world movement of which today there are over 600,000 million Spirit-filled believers.

Frank Bartleman, who chronicled the 1906 revival in Azusa Street, said that this worldwide revival 'was rocked in the cradle of little Wales,' 'brought up in India' and became 'full grown in Los Angeles.'(36) A year later in Britain 1907 it all centred on the parish of All Saints' in Sunderland with its vicar Alexander Alfred Boddy and his wife and ministry partner, Mary.

They speak in tongues

Following a series of meetings from September 1st 1907 led by Norwegian revivalist, Thomas Ball Barratt, the Holy Spirit was poured out with the sign of tongues. By October the Newcastle Chronicle (October 4th 1907) (37) reported:

The meetings are attracting widespread interest. Two meetings are held each day...and these are crowded. [They] are conducted on the lines of a revival meeting...it is not an uncommon spectacle for [the worshippers] to throw themselves on the ground in a paroxysm of weeping, while others gabble and utter what appear to be unintelligible sounds.

A well for Britain

By the end of the year, reports were appearing in the national press.

People were travelling to this newly opened well and going back to their communities carrying the flames of revival and starting their own Pentecostal meetings. The characteristic of this revival, the baptism of the Holy Spirit accompanied by tongues, was highly transferable.

There were annual five-day revivalist gatherings at Sunderland called 'the Sunderland Conventions' which fuelled the fire while the monthly magazine Confidence disseminated the message (38). Regular conventions all round Britain called on key Pentecostal speakers of the day and stoked the flames. There was an emphasis on healing and the pages of Confidence are full of healing testimonies.

Britain's Pentecostal Missionary Union (PMU) was established in 1909. Many young men and women were willing to give their lives for the sake of the gospel, believing the time was short for the coming of the Lord. They also believed that the raison d'etre of the baptism of the Holy Spirit with the accompanying gift of tongues was missions (see Chapter 8). This initial phase of the revival came to an end in 1914 as the Great War devastated Europe.

Hebrides 1949-52
For three years a revival swept Lewis and Harris which make up the largest islands of the Outer Hebrides off the coast of North West Scotland. There was hope that it would spread to the rest of the British Isles, but it remained localised in the Gaelic-speaking community of subsistence farmers and crofters, where no one escaped as the presence of the Lord descended (see Chapter 7).

From small beginnings
It began in the tiny parish of Barvas with two elderly ladies praying twice a week through the night for revival. The scripture that gripped them was, 'I will pour water on the thirsty land, and streams on the dry ground' (Isaiah 44:3). They declared, 'We are dealing with a covenant-keeping God.' (39) And we still are.

One had a vision of what the coming revival would look like, and encouraged by this, seven men met in a barn to pray twice a week. After several months, one young man felt led to read from Psalm 24:3-5, 'Who may ascend the hill of the Lord? Who may stand in his holy place? He who has clean hands and a pure heart...He will receive blessing from the Lord.' He stood and raised his hands to heaven and prayed. At that moment something happened in the barn. God's holiness descended and a power was let loose that shook the parish – but that was just the beginning.

God swept in

Duncan Campbell, the man Peggy had seen in a vision, was sent for. On his first evening in the local Presbyterian church the service was very ordinary, but something happened as he left the building. He said,

When I went to the door of the church I saw a congregation of approximately 600 people. Where had they come from? What had happened? I believe that very night God swept in Pentecostal power, the power of the Holy Ghost. And what happened in the early days of the apostles was happening now in the parish of Barvas. The meeting continued till four in the morning. (40)

Campbell went from parish to parish. Churches crowded day and night became too small, so gatherings took place in the fields. All had revival manifestations of falling down, visions, 'trances' and crying out under deep conviction of sin. Messengers would come from parishes 15 miles away at three in the morning, saying 300 had gathered and were waiting. Work would stop each day at noon for two hours of prayer.

The thing that stands out for me in this revival is what can happen when 'a sense of God lays hold of a community' (see Chapter 7). Three-quarters of the people were born again before ever entering a church. (41) The holiness of God brought men and women to their knees by the roadside. Streams of the young people became missionaries and ministers of the gospel.

And it is just within living memory. The words of Duncan Campbell and other eyewitnesses captured in audio recordings carry the power of this remarkable move of God which can be found with just a little digging on the web.

East Anglia 1921

This little-known revival (42) centred on the fishing town of Lowestoft, affecting other towns in East Anglia and also North East Scotland. People flocked to hear the preaching of Douglas Brown from London, and during the summer of 1921 hundreds came out night after night.

Whole families were converted, and many denominations were involved. Although not as intense as the Hebridean revival, it too was marked by spontaneity, the people just came and Brown said that the predominant feature was the 'felt presence of Christ,'(43) not just in the churches, as whole communities were affected.

Every year there was an invasion of Scottish fisher folk to Lowestoft and Great Yarmouth for the herring season and they carried the revival back to the towns of North East Scotland with the same results.

Never ending

It's not in the scope of this book to examine these revivals in detail and comment on their demise, although I did touch on several ideas why in Chapter 3. Instead, I'll offer the wisdom of revivalists from the 20th century Pentecostal revival. As the revival progressed, Frank Bartleman cautioned, 'Don't steady the ark' (1 Chronicles 13:9). In other words, don't try and touch a move of God to control it; let it go where the Spirit leads. (44)

A.A. Boddy and fellow revivalists saw the Pentecostal movement as the 'birth of the man child' (Revelation 12:1-9) which had to be protected from those who wanted to kill it. He pointed out that revival is not always welcomed, and may well be resisted. This tactic of the enemy needs to be recognised.(45)

Flickering lamps

The First World War (1914-18) was 'history's punctuation mark'(46) and left our nation with a wounded soul. On the eve of war, Foreign Secretary, Sir Edward Grey famously said, 'The lamps are going out all over Europe and we shall not see them lit in our lifetime.'(47) Certainly the revivalist atmosphere of Victorian and Edwardian Britain came to an abrupt halt.

During the inter-war period, the lights flickered again with the remarkable itinerant healing and evangelistic ministry of George Jeffries and that of Smith Wigglesworth as well as the localised revival in East Anglia and eastern Scotland. Then as we have seen, after World War 2 (1939-45), revival swept the Hebrides.

Now entering living memory, the Billy Graham crusades of the 1950s attracted immense crowds. Many churches embraced renewal as waves of the Holy Spirit crashed through all denominational boxes during the charismatic movement of the 1960s and 70s. The new churches emerged and African immigrants brought with them a vibrant spirituality creating huge churches especially in London. Then the revival wave from Toronto hit these shores in 1994. But there has yet to be a national awakening as in the days of Whitefield or Wesley or of the latter 19th and early 20th centuries.

Can it happen again? Yes, I believe it can...

Lord, I have heard of your fame; I stand in awe of your deeds, O Lord.
Renew them in our day, in our time make them known.
Habakkuk 3:2

Endnotes

1. J. Edwin Orr, *The Flaming Tongue*, Moody Press, Chicago, 1973, p ix.

2. Ibid., p 187.

3. I am indebted to Pastor Bill Johnson, Bethel Church, Redding, California, USA for this thought from various talks.

4. www.lollardsociety.org/pdfs/WesleyanConf_WytoWes.pdf

5. William Allen, *The History of Revivals of Religion*, Revival Publishing Company, Co. Antrim, Northern Ireland, 1951, p 21.

6. Susan C. Hyatt, *In the Spirit We're Equal*, Hyatt Press, Dallas, USA, 1998, p 83 and footnote.

7. www.thepotteries.org/dates/census/htm

8. Whittaker, Colin, *Great Revivals*, Marshall, Morgan and Scott, Basingstoke, UK, 1984, p 45.

9. David E. Gardner, *The Trumpet Sounds for Britain*, Jesus is Alive Ministries, England, 2010, p 71.

10. Ibid., p 72.

11. See Chapter 1, endnote xii.

12. A. Skevington Wood, *The Burning Heart*, Cliff College Publishing, Sheffield, 2001, p 116.

13. See Chapter 3, end notes xv, xvi, xvii.

14. http://www.goodreads.com/author/quotes/151350.John_Wesley

15. Skevington Wood, op.cit., pp 197-198.

16. Whittaker, op.cit., pp 61-2.

17. Ibid., p 63.

18. Taylor, Steve, *The Skye Revivals*, New Wine Press, Chichester, UK, 2003, p 115.

19. J. Edwin Orr, *The Second Evangelical Awakening in Britain*, Marshall, Morgan and Scott, London, Edinburgh, UK, 1949, p 207.

20. Ibid. p 38.

21. Ibid. p 17.
22. Ibid., pp 95-101.
23. Ibid., p 99.
24. Based on Matthew 23:19 (KJV)
25. Phoebe Palmer, *Four Years in the Old World*, Foster and Palmer, Jr., New York, USA, 1867, pp 120-147.
26. Kevin Adams and Emyr Jones, *A Pictorial History of Revival*, CWR, Farnham, UK, 2004, p 40.
27. Kevin Adams, *A Diary of Revival*, CWR, Farnham, UK, 2004, p 46.
28. Ibid., p 67.
29. Orr, *The Flaming Tongue*, op.cit., p 6.
30. Ibid., p 11.
31. Colin Whittaker, op.cit., p 96.
32. *Here is Love*, William Rees (1802-1883) translated from Welsh to English by William Edwards in 1900.
33. Orr, *The Flaming Tongue*, op.cit., p 19.
34. Orr, *The Flaming Tongue*, op.cit., p 46.
35. Patrick Dixon, *Signs of Revival*, Kingsway Publications, Eastbourne, UK, 1994, p 164.
36. Frank Bartleman, *Azusa Street*, Bridge-Logos, Gainsville, USA, 1980, p 22 (originally published 1925).
37. www.vision.pwp.blueyonder.co.uk/revival/boddrefs.html
38. A digitised CD of all editions of Confidence from 1908-26 can be obtained from www.revival-library.org/acatalog/pentcoll.html
39. Colin Whittaker, op.cit., p 157-8
40. www.revival-library.org/catalogues/20thcentury/campbell.html
A transcribed message *When the Mountains Flowed Down,* Duncan Campbell.
41. Ibid.
42. Stanley C. Griffin, *A Forgotten Revival*, Day One Publications, Bromley, UK, 1992.
43. Ibid., p 56.
44. Bartleman, op.cit., p 55. Bartleman spent lengthy periods of time in Britain and his letters and articles appear in Confidence.
45. *Confidence*, June 1908, p 17; December 1908, p 27; March 1910, p 68 www.revival-library.org
46. Orr, *The Second Evangelical Awakening*, op.cit., p 9.
47. www.wikipedia.org/wiki/The_lamps_are_going_out

5
Gems in the Rock

O afflicted city, lashed by storms and not comforted, I will build you with stones of turquoise, your foundations with sapphires. I will make your battlements of rubies, your gates of sparkling jewels and all your walls of precious stones. Isaiah 54:11-12

Men and Women of God

Britain has been rich in men and women of God. They have laid our Christian foundations, walked the highways and byways, stopping for the one or for the crowds in order to tell the good news of Jesus. As centuries advanced so methods have changed, but the message is the same. Green fields may have given way to large halls and stadiums, but still crowds have gathered, drawn by the expectation of encountering the divine or maybe just curiosity.

In the 7th century Aidan and Cuthbert and bands of saintly Celtic monks tramped the lanes. In the 13th century the Grey Friars of St Francis followed in their footsteps. John Wycliffe's Lollards in the 14th century were true apostles as they followed the divine call and were sent out around the land. Then there was George Fox and every Friend who refused to stop preaching at the expense of their comfort and freedom. George Whitefield preached to the masses; John Wesley in his lifetime rode a staggering quarter of a million miles on horseback.

We may never know many of their names, but they all deserve honour for their faithfulness and perseverance.

They are forever on God's heart like the gem stones on the breastplate of the high priest in the Old Testament (Exodus 17:15-21).

Revivalists of the modern era

During the 1800s we also had our fair share of evangelists and preachers. There was the nationwide impact of William and Catherine Booth. Henry Grattan Guinness won thousands of converts and trained over one thousand as missionaries. Brownlow North was compared with George Whitefield, David Morgan's preaching awakened Wales, and so many more itinerated across our nation or had a local influence.

As the 19th century dawned, the age of exploration gave way to global trade and colonisation and with this came easier travel and communication. We were visited by revivalists from the States who fuelled the mid-century evangelical awakening we were experiencing and had great successes. Names such as James Caughey, Charles Finney, Robert and Hannah Whitall Smith, Phoebe Palmer, D.L. Moody, and R.A. Torrey were well known. This trans-Atlantic exchange complemented our home-grown revivalists and has continued to this present day.

Our more recent history

Other names stand out in our more recent Christian history. There are Evan Roberts of the 1904 Welsh Revival, Alexander and Mary Boddy who led the Pentecostal revival of 1907-1914, the now legendary Smith Wigglesworth whose remarkable ministry spanned six decades, and healing evangelist George Jeffries who packed the largest halls in the land in the 1920s and 30s. Nor can we exclude the Billy Graham crusades in the 1950s, whose impact will only be known in heaven.

All these men and women ploughed their lives into our soil, and sowed seeds of the gospel the length and breadth of Britain.

Born in the fire

If revivals laid down deposits of gold in the land that makes up the British Isles, then these men and women are the gems in the rock; sapphires, diamonds, rubies whose lives sparkle and add wealth to our nation's history with God. Their ministries were born and forged in the fire of encounter with God and they were never the same again.

Their hearts had been captured and their lives were marked by a holy passion.

John Wesley once told a friend that his brother, Charles Wesley's hymn (1) summed up his Christian experience. It expresses the same depth of passion shared by our other 'gems' and still resonates in hearts today.

O Thou who camest from above
The pure celestial fire to impart
Kindle a flame of sacred love
On the mean altar of my heart!

There let it for Thy glory burn
With inextinguishable blaze;
And trembling to its source return,
With humble prayer and fervent praise.

Jesus, confirm my heart's desire
To work, and speak, and think for Thee;
Still let me guard the holy fire,
And still stir up Thy gift in me.

I can find no better comment than this quotation, 'Guarding the holy fire; that was what he was doing. He was himself a flame going up and down the land, lighting candles such as by God's grace, would never be put out...never waning, never smoky, darting from point to point, lighting up the whole kingdom...' (2)

What richness there still is in these words which challenge us to guard the holy fire inside us.

Never the same again

Common to these revivalists was a depth of spiritual encounter. Each could point you to a time in their lives after which nothing could ever be the same again. Words are powerful, not just spoken words but written ones as well and their own descriptions of these moments still carry the life of the Spirit just as if they were on the breath of the person who spoke them. For this reason I will use their own words to describe their encounters with the divine. These encounters led to their greatness and ring down through the ages fresh with life and power.

George Fox – a man for his generation

George Fox was a man marked by a series of divine encounters and he responded by giving his life for the cause of Christ. Nothing could steer him off course. His life reads like that of the Apostle Paul who said, 'None of these things move me, nor neither do I count my life dear to myself, so that I may finish my race with joy, and the ministry which I received from the Lord Jesus, to testify to the gospel of the grace of God.' (Acts 20:24, NKJV) The following entry from his journal holds one of the clues to his endurance. (3)

Now I came up in spirit through the flaming sword, into the paradise of God. All things were new; and all creation gave unto me another smell than before, beyond what words can utter. I knew nothing but pureness, and innocency, and righteousness; being renewed into the image of God by Jesus Christ, to the state of Adam, which he was in before he fell. The creation was opened to me; and it was showed me how all things had their names given them according to their nature and virtue...And the Lord showed me that such as were faithful to Him, in the power and light of Christ, should come up into that state in which Adam was before he fell.

Could it be that while suffering in the darkest dungeons, he was able to go back to this time in the Spirit and receive strength to sustain him? A thought to ponder...

Living from heaven to earth

His life was lived from heaven to earth. Once after being severely beaten for his faith, he recalled, 'I was lying in a watery common, and the people standing about me, I lay still a little while, and the power of the Lord sprang through me, and the eternal refreshings revived me; so that I stood up again in the strengthening power of the eternal God and stretching out my arms among them, I said, with a loud voice, 'Strike again; here are my arms, my head, and my cheeks.'(4)

A positive mystic

Fox was a prophet to his generation. He had regular audiences with Oliver Cromwell who came to have the utmost respect for him, even though Fox always declared the truth and was in no way intimidated by the nation's ruler. He foresaw national events such as the Great Plague of 1665 and the Fire of London in 1666, as well issues concerning foreign policy. He wrote,

...many came to me...and the Lord's power brake forth; and I had great openings and prophesies; and spake unto them of the things of God, and they heard with attention and silence, and went away, and spread the fame thereof. (5)

Fox could be described as a 'positive mystic' (6) because his experiences of God's presence caused him to engage intensely with life rather than withdraw from it. We will see in Chapter 8 that reforms led by Quakers have helped change the face of Britain. He was true revivalist, a man of the Spirit but also of the word. One Friend said, 'Though the Bible were lost, it might be found in the mouth of George Fox.'(7)

John Wesley – the presence of his majesty

A strong sense of destiny rested on John Wesley. At the age of five he was rescued from a fire at the rectory where he lived. He always said he was 'a brand plucked from the burning' (Zechariah 3:2) and believed he had been saved for a purpose, as did his godly mother Susanna. He strove to ingratiate himself to God through good works, but everything changed after his heart was 'strangely warmed' and emotion entered his Christian experience at the Aldersgate meeting in May 1738.

Another encounter followed which George Whitefield and his brother Charles shared. It was at an all-night prayer meeting of Anglican clergy as they met to usher in the New Year of 1739.

About three in the morning as we were continuing instant in prayer, the power of God came mightily upon us, insomuch that many cried out for exceeding joy, and many fell to the ground. As soon as we were recovered a little from that awe and amazement at the presence of his Majesty, we broke out with one voice, 'We praise thee O God, we acknowledge thee to be the Lord.'(8)

The presence never left him, and it was after this that his real ministry began. The key to his inner life with God was found in the way he would sit with an open Bible: Here then I am, far from the busy ways of men. I sit down alone: only God is here. In his presence I open, I read His book; for this end, to find the way to heaven...And what I thus learn I teach. (9) The hours of four to five in the morning would find him on his knees. All Britain benefited from what he heard in those encounters from heaven.

Charles Finney – waves of liquid love

Riding the crest of the mid-19th century transatlantic revivals was converted lawyer Charles Finney (1792-1873). He conducted revival meetings in England in 1849 and later in England and Scotland in 1858-9. Thousands were touched by his fire as he would 'plead God's case to an unbelieving world.' His power can be traced back to this moment in time:

Without any expectation of it, without ever having the thought in my mind that there was any such thing for me, the Holy Spirit descended on me in a manner that seemed to go through me body and soul. I could feel the impression like a wave of electricity going through and through me. Indeed it seemed to come in waves and waves of liquid love for I could not express it in any other way, it seemed the very breath of God. I can recollect that it seemed to fan me like immense wings. No words can express the wonderful love that was shed abroad in my heart. I wept aloud with joy and love and I do not know but I should say I literally bellowed out the unutterable gushings of my heart. (10)

D.L. Moody's sacred experience

In 1873, American evangelist D.L. Moody (1837–1899) took Britain by storm over two years as he preached to huge crowds in many major cities. In London alone over a twenty-week period he preached to two-and-a-half million people. It was the first of several visits.

One revival historian said that 'his work in Britain places him high in the list of the spiritual makers of modern Britain.'(11) It all began one day... I was crying all the time that God would fill me with his Spirit. Well, one day, in the city of New York – oh what a day! I cannot describe it, I seldom refer to it; it is almost too sacred an experience to name. Paul had an experience of which he never spoke for fourteen years. I can only say that God revealed himself to me, and I had such an experience of his love that I had to ask him to stay his hand. I went to preaching again. The sermons were not different; I did not present any new truths, and yet hundreds were converted. I would not be placed back where I was before that blessed experience for all the world. (12)

William Booth – God had all there was

As for William Booth, late in life he talked about the secret of his success. One evening when walking home from chapel, aged 15, he dedicated his life to God. He promised, 'God shall have all there is of William Booth.' A simple encounter, yet so profound and a promise he never recanted.

There have been men with greater brains than I, men with greater opportunities. But from the day I got the poor of London on my heart and caught a vision of all Jesus Christ could do with them, on that day I made up my mind that God would have all of William Booth there was. And if there is anything of power in the Salvation Army today, it is because God has had all the adoration of my heart, all the power of my will, and all the influence of my life. (13)

Smith Wigglesworth – baptised in the Holy Spirit

Although he was a seasoned open-air evangelist, when it came to preaching in Bowland Street Mission, Bradford, Yorkshire which he led with his wife, Polly, Smith Wigglesworth was tongue-tied. He preferred sitting on the back row looking after the children while his wife Polly preached, that is until he was baptised in the Holy Spirit on 28th October 1907.

He had travelled to Sunderland after hearing that the Holy Spirit was being poured out there in a remarkable way and that people were speaking in tongues. He described what happened in a letter to *Confidence*. (14)

I came to Sunderland with a holy, breathing cry after this clear manifestation [tongues]. At about 11 a.m. Tuesday morning at All Saints' Vicarage, I asked a sister to help me to the witness of the baptism of the Holy Ghost. She laid hands on me in the presence of a brother. The fire fell and burned in me till the Holy Spirit revealed absolute purity before God... A marvellous revelation took place, my body became full of light and holy presence, and in the revelation I saw an empty cross and at the same time the Jesus I loved and adored, crowned in the glory in a reigning position. The glorious remembrance of these moments is beyond my expression to give.

When I could not find words to express, then an irresistible power filled me and moved my being till I found to my glorious astonishment I was speaking in other tongues clearly. After this a burning love for everybody filled my soul.

No longer tongue-tied, he returned to the mission and preached fluently under a heavy anointing the very next Sunday. He said, 'Suddenly I felt that I had prophetic utterances which were flowing like a river by the power of the Holy Spirit.' His surprised wife summed it up, 'That's not my Smith...What's happened to the man!'(15) What had happened was an encounter with God that changed the course of Smith's life and was to change the lives of probably millions that came under the influence of his ministry.

Evan Roberts – face to face with God

Evan Roberts had a passionate hunger for revival in Wales. He wrote to a friend, 'For ten or eleven years, I have prayed for revival. I could sit up all night to read or talk about revivals. It was the Spirit that moved me to think about a revival.'(16) He recalls that after praying for 11 years:

I was taken up into a great expanse – without time and space. It was communion with God. I found myself with unspeakable joy and awe in the very presence of the almighty God. I was privileged to speak face to face with him as a man speaks face to face with a friend. Before this, a far-off God I had. I was frightened that night, but never since. So great was my shivering that I rocked the bed, and, my brother, being awakened, took hold of me thinking I was ill.

After that experience I was awakened every night a little after one o' clock...What it was I cannot tell you, except that it was divine. I felt it and it seemed to change all my nature and I saw things in a different light and I knew that God was going to work in the land and not only this land but in all the world. About five o'clock I was again allowed to sleep on till about nine. (17)

Evan Roberts ministered as a man who encountered heaven. Then revival came following the other power encounter with the Spirit of God he had at the meeting in Blaenannerch (Chapter 4).

George Jeffries – an inflow of divine life

We'll be looking in more detail at Welsh-born George Jeffries' remarkable healing ministry in the next chapter, but knowing he had been called to preach, it seemed an impossibility to the young George. This was because of a creeping paralysis that affected his speech, that is, until his encounter with God. (18)

We were kneeling in prayer one Sunday morning and were interceding... it was exactly nine o'clock when the power of God came upon me and I received such an inflow of divine life that I can only liken the experience to being charged with electricity. It seemed as if my head were connected to a most powerful electric battery. My whole body from head to foot was quickened by the Spirit of God and I was healed.

The Lord's hand rested strongly upon him and he preached to some of the largest audiences known in Britain. He confessed, 'I have been confronted by monster congregations and if it were not for the frequent quickening of the Holy Spirit, I would have been helpless.'

The word in their hearts

Is not my word like a fire, declares the Lord, and like a hammer that breaks a rock in pieces? (Jeremiah 23:29)

All these revivalists carried the word like fire in their hearts. For Phoebe Palmer, as for many, it was an encounter with a revealed word of truth as well as the Spirit that motivated them. A teacher and preacher of holiness, Phoebe desperately wanted to know for certain whether she had received the gift of sanctification. Feelings came and went and she felt she couldn't base her faith on them.

Then one day after months of seeking God she came to her 'naked faith in the naked word' experience. As she laid all on the altar, she believed that the fire of God would consume the sacrifice by faith (Matthew 23:19 KJV). She taught her 'altar theology' around Britain from 1859-63 and as well as making 17,000 converts, many more were sanctified. She was also a theologian and a forerunner of Pentecostal theology.

On a personal note, she is my heroine and deserves a much higher profile in Britain's history with God. Her quaintly named book, *Four Years in the Old World*, chronicles her travels around Britain and is inspirational.

The Prince of Preachers
It was the oratory of the evangelistic preachers of the 18th and 19th century that broke the rock in pieces for many.

Opposite the multicultural market of the Elephant and Castle area in London is the imposing Metropolitan Tabernacle. It was built in 1898 to house the 6,000 people who came every Sunday to hear the 'Prince of Preachers,' Charles Haddon Spurgeon.

Born a Methodist, Spurgeon become a Baptist and pastored a church from the age of 20. On occasions when this was too small, he would hire a big London music hall that seated 10,000 people. It is said that in his lifetime he preached to over 10 million and many of his sermons were published.

Alexander Boddy – chasing revival
Boddy chased revival and found it...or rather it found him.

Like many great men and women of God, Revd. Alexander Boddy seemed to live outside of his time. Not content to be a parochial vicar, he was a member of the Royal Geographical Society and travelled around the world.

A man of daring and adventure, he chased revival along with his wife, Mary, who attended the annual Keswick Conventions with him.

When he heard about the Welsh Revival, Boddy went there and ministered with Evan Roberts at 'the most spiritual and wonderful gatherings.' Nevertheless he was convinced that 'the Lord always has something better beyond.' Carrying a prophecy from Evan in his heart that 'the Holy Spirit is going to fall upon you...the power of God will sweep over Sunderland,' he returned home and gathered together a company of men who met night after night to pray for an outpouring of the Spirit.(19) Hearing that a Pentecostal revival had broken out in Christiana (Oslo), Norway under the leadership of Thomas Barratt, Boddy went there and found a presence and power even beyond what he had experienced in Wales. He was willing to face ridicule from other Christian leaders to embrace the new thing God was doing. This made room for the Holy Spirit to have his way from the very first day of the outpouring in Sunderland, September 1st 1907.

As for his own Holy Spirit baptism, Boddy wrote of the encounter, 'I hope that precious memory of the glorious Spirit-filled meeting on Monday December 2nd 1907 will never fade away...I was prostrated before the Lord, feeling that I could not get low enough...as I lay before the Lord, he took my tongue as I yielded and obeyed; first speaking quickly but quietly and then more powerfully...' (20)

Loved by parishioners and visitors alike, Boddy and his wife stewarded the revival well for seven years; they knew how to host the presence. They provided a platform for men and women who were carrying the fire. Both he and Mary gave a theology regarding the distinctives of Spirit baptism and healing through their writings and messages.

Several years into the revival he commented, 'The Lord Jesus was and is the centre of our teaching and worship at Sunderland. Surely this has been the secret of blessing, and we think it is the one reason for his willingness to use this place.'(21)

Revival in the blood
As in a natural family, the wider spiritual environment is a cradle to nurture what we are carrying spiritually, at least initially.

Looking at the lives of these revivalists, it's interesting to know when and where they were born, born again or when vision was birthed in them, what influences there were on their lives. It gives a clue as to what God had deposited in them. It will also help us understand what we ourselves are carrying and what's in our spiritual DNA as we look back over our lives in the same way. Here are just a few examples.

Charles Finney was born a year after Wesley's death in 1792. Smith Wigglesworth was born in the year of revivals, 1859. He was reborn, aged 8, in a Methodist revival meeting and during his early life had the direct influences of the Church of England, Plymouth Brethren, the holiness and healing Movements, the Salvation Army as well as the

Methodists!(22) Evan Roberts was born in the aftermath of the second evangelical awakening in 1878.

Moody's ministry was a product of the same awakening.

Mary Boddy, just as much a revivalist as her husband Alexander, was a descendant of Wesley's wife, Mary Vazielle, and gave that distinct name to her children. Polly Wigglesworth, partner in marriage and ministry to Smith, was baptised by healer, James Alexander Dowie in the Albert Hall, London, in 1900 and was an active member of the Holiness and Healing movement. (23)

George and Stephen Jeffries were born again at the beginning of the Welsh Revival in 1904. George was 15 and Stephen 28. George Jeffries took revival out of the cradle of Wales, maturing in his ministry and impacting Britain and inspiring a new generation.

It's interesting that Stephen's son Edward became a powerful healing evangelist. He held huge meetings across the country in the 1930s, climaxing in the Liverpool Tent Revival of 1934. This lasted over 17 weeks with tens of thousands in attendance daily and was accompanied by salvations and remarkable healings. Revival was certainly in the blood of the Jeffries family!

Role models

Christian role models not only inspire but give permission to be radical followers of Christ. All Catherine Booth needed was a female role model to propel her into her destiny. In the 19th century it was not considered proper for a woman to have a public preaching ministry, so when she heard Phoebe Palmer she was delighted and felt a release in her spirit.

One Sunday morning in 1860, Catherine announced that she would speak that evening at the church led by her husband. That night she preached to a full house, with people sitting on the windowsills. William was delighted and Catherine developed a reputation as an outstanding preacher.

As a role model herself, Catherine led the way for others and the Salvation Army became noted for its equality in ministry. In fact, Booth once quipped, 'My best men are women!'(24) It was all because of a role model that gave her permission to be who she was called to be.

Heroes

William Booth himself began his ministry by copying his hero, John Wesley who preached to the poor in the open air. He would stand on a chair outside his rented house in Nottingham and sing and speak urging his listeners to go into a room in his house to get right with God. But hearing evangelist James Caughey speak night after night in 1846 at a chapel in Nottingham, further stirred Booth's desire to see souls saved.

The role models and those following them came together at several large gatherings in Birmingham in 1863, when Phoebe Palmer was followed by the Booths who were in turn followed by James Caughey. During that year the city was thoroughly evangelised; it didn't stand a chance!

It's clear we don't live just to ourselves. Looking back I can see influences from the 'cradle' I was nurtured in, as well as other seedbeds of faith, and I am richer for them. I'm so grateful for men and women of God who have shaped my life.

And mantles

Sometimes there is a clear impartation from an individual which forever changes someone's life. In chapter 10 I will be exploring this from a biblical standpoint when we consider the lives of Elijah and Elisha.

A great mantle of prophetic anointing came upon George Fox following the death of an old, unknown, prophet called Brown. Before his death he had asked to speak to Fox, and prophesied over him about his future ministry. (25)

In more recent times, a similar event happened to evangelist Reinhart Bonnke. In 1962 he had finished his Bible School training in Wales and was spending an afternoon in London before going back home to Germany. He found himself outside the house of the healing evangelist George Jeffries, aware that for several decades in the first part of the 20th century he had an amazing ministry of signs and wonders in Britain.

Taking courage he knocked on the door, and the now old and fragile Jeffries prayed for him as he knelt down. He left and the next day he heard that George Jeffries had passed from this life. Bonnke said of this encounter, 'I've caught a mantle...That day the baton and flame met and I'm still running.'(26)

For the sake of the gospel

Nearly every revivalist faced opposition or heartache of some sort, yet they tenaciously held on to what they believed. Fox was imprisoned, Wesley faced the mobs, Booth was pelted with rotten fruit and eggs, Evan Roberts was charged with sheer emotionalism and was written against, and Boddy was told that tongues are from the devil. Phoebe Palmer lost three of her five children in infancy but continued with her ministry.

Each has a human story to tell because they were human beings. Yet they lived as spiritual beings having an earthly experience rather than human beings having a spiritual experience. There's a world of difference.

What makes a revivalist?

All these lives were characterised by remarkable success and show what can be achieved when human beings partner with heaven. Their impact was more than is naturally possible for one man or woman.

Looking at the lives of these gems, what are the common characteristics? Passion, hunger, prayer, vision, spiritual power, chasing after God, dedication, being led by the Spirit, valuing the presence, being men and women of the Word, stewarding revelation...the list goes on; the results, staggering.

It's easy to come away with the impression that God only uses superhuman heroes and heroines so I want to end with the story of Peggy and Christine.

The story of Peggy and Christine

Nothing can disqualify you for becoming a revivalist. You may feel like one of those 'weak parts' mentioned in 1 Corinthians 12, but remember Paul goes on to say that they are indispensable.

I have an old, faded photograph of Peggy and Christine Smith wrapped in shawls looking as if they belonged in some century long ago. Peggy was 84 years old and blind, and Christine, 82, was doubled up with arthritis. In 1949 they lived in a small stone cottage on the Isle of Lewis in the Hebrides.

Old and frail, they still carried revival in their hearts. Twice a week they would get on their knees at 10 o'clock at night and pray until 4 in the morning. In a vision Peggy saw revival once again sweep the Hebrides and the man God was going to use, Duncan Campbell. She asked her minister to contact him and gather the church to pray, and as we have seen, revival did indeed break out.

One day Peggy sent for Campbell and told him to go to a certain village because she had 'seen' seven men who would be converted. He didn't feel any leading but old Peggy gently rebuked him in her native Gaelic, 'Mr. Campbell, if you were living as near to God as you ought to be, he would reveal his secrets to you also.'(27)

So he went and sure enough the men were there and responded to the gospel. Unable to leave the cottage, the sisters prayed for all the families on the island. They just spent hours in his presence and knew intimacy with God, the key to all fruitfulness.

Their stories are written in heaven's scroll of remembrance alongside the Wesleys and the Wigglesworths. Ours can be too.

Cheering us on

I've written about just a few of the men and women who comprise that great cloud of witnesses cheering us on from the grandstands of heaven. Every one of them is a gem, precious to God's heart and also part of our spiritual ancestry. What they carried is our spiritual inheritance.

Theirs may have been an unfinished race. Someone may be required to pick up their baton and run again. Others may provide an example or inspire us to run the particular race that God had given us. Whatever the case, let this be our response...

Therefore, since we are surrounded by such a great cloud of witnesses, let us throw off everything that hinders and the sin that so easily entangles, and let us run with perseverance that race marked out for us. Let us fix our eyes on Jesus, the author and perfecter of our faith.
Hebrews 12:1, 2

Endnotes
1. Charles Wesley, *O Thou Who Camest From Above*, 1762.

2. A. Skevington Wood, *The Burning Heart*, Cliff College Publishing, Sheffield, UK, 2001, p 68.

3. Jeff Doles, *Miracles and Manifestations of the Holy Spirit in the History of the Church*, Walking Barefoot Ministries. Florida, USA, 2008, p 187. Quoting from Fox's Journal, Chapter 2.

4. Edmund Goerke, *The Gift of Healing in the Life of George Fox*, www.quakerinfo.com/healing1.shtml.

5. Patrick Dixon, *Signs of Revival*, Eastbourne, UK, 1994, p 309.

6. Susan Hyatt, *In the Spirit We're Equal*, Hyatt Press, Dallas, USA, 1998, p 95.

7. Ibid., p 96.

8. Eddie Hyatt, *2000 Years of Charismatic Christianity*, Hyatt International Ministries, Dallas, USA, 1998, p 108. See also Chapters 3 and 4 of this book.

9. A Skevington Wood, op.cit., p 211.

10. Roberts Liardon, *God's Generals, The Revivalists*, Whitaker House, USA, 2008, p 295.

11. J Edwin Orr, *The Second Evangelical Awakening in Britain*, Marshall, Morgan and Scott, London, Edinburgh, UK, 1949, p 244.

12. Eddie Hyatt, op.cit., p 142.

13. www.gospeltruth.net/booth/booth_index.htm.

14. *Confidence*, 1908, p 15.

15. Frodsham, Stanley, *Apostle of Faith*, Gospel Publishing House, Springfield USA, 1993, p 47.

16. J. Edwin Orr, *The Flaming Tongue*, Moody Press, Chicago, USA, 1973, p 4.

17. Kevin Adams, *Diary of a Revival*, CWR, Farnham, U.K., 2004, pp 41-2.

18. Jeffries, George, *Healing Rays*, pp 56-7. First published 1932. www.revival-library.org

19. Confidence, August 1910, p 193.

20. William K. Kay, *Inside Story*, Mattersey Hall Publishing, Mattersey. UK, 1990, pp 24-5.

21. *Confidence*, August 1910, p 193.

22. Frodsham, op.cit., p119.

23. Diana Chapman, *Searching the Source of the River*, Push Publishing, London, UK, p 162.

24. http://www1.salvationarmy.org.uk/uki/www_uki_ihc.nsf/stc-vw-sublinks/80D68 E44B63B7355802574FD00300DF1?openDocument

25. Roberts Liardon, *God's Generals, The Roaring Reformers*, Whitaker House, New Kensington, USA, 2003, p 351.

26. Chapman, op.cit., p 175.

27. Colin Whittaker, *Great Revivals*, Marshall, Morgan and Scott, Basingstoke, UK, 1984, p 161.

6
Signs That Make You Wonder

Jesus of Nazareth was a man accredited by God to you by miracles, wonders and signs which God did among you through him. Acts 2:22

A supernatural stream

Signs and wonders are in our foundations. They were part and parcel of the message of salvation carried to this country and so 'the English (and Irish, Scottish and Welsh) by outward miracles were drawn to inward grace.'(1) Just as Jesus was accredited by God by 'miracles, wonders and signs,' he accredited his disciples in the same way. So it shouldn't surprise us to read of a supernatural stream in Britain that runs through history to the present day.

Driving out demons, speaking in new tongues, healings, wonders in the heavens above and signs on the earth below (Mark 16:17 and Acts 2:19) are all part of this stream. It's difficult to know how many drunk poison and lived, and as for handling snakes the nearest we get to that is the legend surrounding St. Patrick who was said to have banished snakes from Ireland; probably symbolic for driving out the old, pagan ways. But this chapter gives a taste of Britain's history with a supernatural God.

Miracles in the cradle

Where the Holy Spirit has been welcomed and Jesus glorified, signs have accompanied believers of all persuasions and in all ages. It has been no more so than at times of revival and when revelation of truth birthed new denominations.

A.J. Gordon got it right when he commented,

Whenever we find a revival of primitive faith and apostolic simplicity, there we find a profession of the chaste and evangelical miracles which characterized the apostolic age. These attend the cradle of every spiritual reformation, as they did the birth of the church herself. (2)

Written in the journals

We are very fortunate that we can still read the journals of George Fox and John Wesley. They are overflowing with miracles, signs and wonders.

If any Quakers or Methodists are reading this, I challenge you to get hold of the books your founding father wrote. They contain your heritage, and the supernatural contained in them was never meant to end but to cascade down the generations. They are not written as hagiographies, as were the lives of the saints, but as factual, day-to-day accounts of what happens when heaven draws near, dated and attested to.

They quaked in his presence

Quakers: their very name tells you there was something supernatural about this group of people. When the Holy Spirit fell on them, they trembled in his presence. 'Some would swoon as "with epilepsy," and while lips quivered and hands shook, the worshippers might lie on the ground in this condition for hours at a time.'(3)

And it was not only the people that quaked! George Fox once wrote about a time he was at Mansfield, '[It was] a great meeting of professors [Christians] and people; and I was moved to pray; and the Lord's power was so great, that the house seemed to be shaken. When I had done, some of the professors said, 'It was now as in the days of the apostles, when the house was shaken where they were.'(4)

A book of miracles

The Quakers believed in the outpouring of the Holy Spirit and speaking in tongues like the Pentecostals three centuries later. There were healings, miracles, prophesies, discerning of spirits, and deliverances. The list of the supernatural in their midst is endless.

There were also manifestations that we associate with revivals. Fox's Journal published in 1694 is full of the supernatural as is Fox's Book of Miracles which Friends published after his death to show what was 'wrought by heavenly power in those days.' Both are available today and make inspiring reading.

Give God the glory

There are so many stories to tell. I have chosen this one because it gives us a glimpse of the gentle heart of the man, Fox.

One Friend called John had a pain in his arm and hand that had totally incapacitated him for three months. In a vision he saw Fox laying his hand on his shoulder and all the pain left. He sought Fox out and as they walked together Fox put his hand on his shoulder and said, 'The Lord strengthen thee both within and without.'

The next day John went home with his 'hand and arm restored to former use and strength, without any pain.' The next time they met, Fox said, 'John, thou mended, thou mended?' John answered, 'Yes, very well in a little time.' 'Well', said he, 'give God the glory.'(5)

Remarkable!

In one of the most remarkable miracles I have read about, Fox was in Maryland, New England with a friend John Jay who fell off his horse and broke his neck. He was dead as far as everyone was concerned. Fox got hold of his hair and turned his limp head in all directions before putting one hand under the chin and another behind the head as he used all his strength to raise the head up and firmly put it back in place. He records, 'I soon perceived his neck began to grow stiff again, and then he began to rattle in his throat, and quickly after to breathe.' After food and a rest, John began to speak. Fox records that the people who saw this miracle were amazed! The next day he was on the saddle again and rode 16 miles, and 'thereafter many hundreds of miles.'(6)

The 'enthusiastic' Methodists

John Wesley and those like him were called 'enthusiasts.' It was not a complimentary term in those days; it meant that you had just gone too far in regard to your religion! It is difficult to know what examples to give of the miracles of healing and deliverances that accompanied Wesley because there are so many.

Wesley was healed himself on numerous occasions and at one time his horse was healed at the same time! 'My horse was exceeding lame...I was thoroughly tired, and my head ached more than it had done for some months...I then thought, "Cannot God heal either man or beast?"...Immediately my headache ceased, and my horse's lameness in the same instant. Nor did he halt any more either that day or the next.'(7)

Here's another story from his journal. 'Mr. Meyrick could not live over the night...his legs being cold and (as it seemed) dead already... we called upon God...He opened his eyes...and from that hour, he continued to recover his strength, till he was restored to perfect health.'(8)

Wesley wrote, 'So many living witnesses hath God given that his hand is still "stretched out to heal" and that "signs and wonders are even now wrought by his holy child Jesus."(9)

Spiritual influenza

Wesley frequently described in vivid detail what happened when he preached. At Newgate prison, Bristol, he commented, 'immediately one and another, and another sunk to the earth: They dropped on every side thunderstruck.' (10) Wesley often described people crying out 'in agonies of death' as they were under conviction of sin.

Regarding the revival in Everton, Norfolk there were so many bizarre manifestations when Revd. Berridge was preaching in May 1759 that 'a stranger coming to Everton, and knowing nothing about the "spiritual influenza," would have thought he had come to a place where every other man was a lunatic or a drunkard!'(11)

As Wesley stood on a chair watching the proceedings there was 'a mixture of various sounds; some shrieking, some roaring aloud. The most general was a loud breathing, like that of people half strangled and gasping for life. And indeed almost all the cries were like those of human creatures dying in bitter anguish. Great numbers wept without any noise; others fell down as dead; some sinking into silence; some with extreme noise and violent agitation.'(12)

Wesley's wisdom
A few months later Wesley revisited this group of people and found them 'refreshed with the multitude of peace.' Still grappling with the scenes he had witnessed previously, he offered his wisdom,

The danger was to regard extraordinary circumstances too much...as if these were essential to inward work, so that it could not go on without them.

Perhaps the danger is to regard them too little; to condemn them altogether; to imagine they had nothing of God in them; yea, were a hindrance to the work: Whereas the truth is, God suddenly and strongly convinced many that they were undone, lost sinners; the natural consequences whereof were sudden outcries, and strong bodily convulsions.

He also comments that some manifestations are 'nature mixed with grace' or Satan mimicking this part of the work of God to discredit it.'(13)

Other entries in his journal show that others 'dropped down and lay as dead' for hours because they were so filled with the love of God, and were unable to go to work! (14)

God's work, God's way
Whitefield objected to these manifestations and was talking to his friend Wesley about it one day in 1739. The next day as Whitefield himself was preaching, 'four persons sunk down close to him...one of them lay without either sense or motion. A second trembled exceedingly. The third had strong convulsions all over his body, but made no noise, unless by groans. The forth, equally convulsed, called upon God, with strong cries and tears.'

Wesley commented that 'from this time, I trust, we shall all suffer God to carry on his work in the way that pleaseth him.'(15) He called it 'a miserable mistake' when it was thought that the gifts were just for an apostolic age, it was just that 'the love of many had waxed cold' and when he [Jesus] came to examine his church, he couldn't 'find faith on the earth.'(16)

Magic Methodists

As well as the Primitive Methodists keeping the 'signs and wonders' of Wesley's Methodism alive, there were also a group curiously called the 'Magic Methodists' of Delamere Forest, Cheshire, so named because of so many supernatural occurrences associated with them.

Led by James Crawford, his disciples were noted for their visions and dreams and they saw many healings though the laying on of hands. His small cottage was called 'the College' as people would gather there around him to learn from the Holy Spirit.

Miracles on the margins

Dotted in and around our history are so many more instances of the supernatural. In the latter part of the 17th century, the Huguenots, Protestants from France who were exiled in England, 'carried here and there the lost art of supernatural healing.'(17)   At the same time the Scottish Covenanters, who wanted to keep the Church of Scotland free from English interference, saw many miracles. One John Welch prayed over the body of a young man for 48 hours 'til he was 'cold dead' then begged for one more hour until life entered him. (18)

There have always been skeptics from the ranks of the institutional church. In relation to the collection of miracles amongst the Covenanters one author wrote,

Some may be ready to object that many things related to this collection smell too much of enthusiasm; and that other things narrated therein are beyond all credit. But these we must suppose to be either quite ignorant of what the Lord did for our forefathers in former times, or else, in a great measure, destitute of the like gracious influences of the Holy Spirit by which they were actuated and animated.(19)

Demonstrating God in the Hebrides

I love what Duncan Campbell said regarding the revival in the Hebrides,

Miracles, supernatural, beyond human explanation – it's God. And I am fully persuaded...that unless we see something like this happening the average man will stagger back from our efforts, our conferences, conventions and crusades – they will stagger back disappointed, disillusioned and despairing. But oh, if something happens that demonstrates God! (20)

And that's exactly what did happen on the remote Outer Hebrides in the mid 20th century. There were no tongues or recorded healings but 'men [were] brought face to face with the holiness of God'. When heaven comes down, the supernatural cannot be contained and no persuasion is needed for men to get back into a right relationship with God. What else would make a secondary school headmaster lay on his face crying as he is led to the Lord by two of his 15-year-old pupils who had been saved the night before?

Duncan Campbell would find men face down in trances before their weaving looms before he even entered the house. Men and women came under deep conviction and were captivated by the reality of heaven.

In one village a blacksmith remembered God's promise, 'I will pour water upon him who is thirsty' (Isaiah 44:3, KJV) and boldly prayed, 'God, I now take upon myself to challenge you to fulfil your covenant engagement.' The whole house shook Acts 4 style, the dishes shook and a jug fell off the dresser. Not surprisingly, revival came to that village.

God demonstrated who he is!

Holy laughter

After Smith Wigglesworth returned home from his Holy Spirit encounter in Sunderland he was a different man. The first Sunday back at the Bowland Street Mission in Bradford, he preached with power. Following the word, many of the congregation including himself and his wife, Polly found themselves rolling around on the floor laughing.

Wesley himself experienced holy laughter but was uncertain what to make of it. Writing about an experience he had in 1729 he said,

Part of Sunday my brother and I then used to spend in walking in meadows and singing psalms. But one day, just as we were beginning to sing, he burst out in loud laughter. I asked him if he were distracted; and I began to be very angry and presently after to laugh as loud as he. Nor could we possibly refrain, through we were ready to tear ourselves in pieces, but were forced to go home without singing another line. (21)

All things weird and wonderful

In the 1859 revival in Northern Ireland there were instances of people not just being 'struck down in their scores' but many who for a while become deaf or dumb (like Zechariah) or blind (like Paul) as well as having extraordinary visions.(22) As you can imagine, these signs did make people wonder!

One medical doctor commented, 'They look for revival, but will not accept it unless it tallies with their own pre-conceived opinions.' Interestingly he continued to say that the revival had taken root in Coleraine more than anywhere else because the clergy of all denominations had allowed the manifestations to 'progress without interruption.' More people were converted in that place in four months than in the previous fifty years.

Manifestations of some sort or another are common to all revivals Regarding one meeting during the Welsh Revival, an eyewitness said, 'If you put a man in the midst of one of these meetings who knows nothing of the language of the Spirit, and nothing of the life of the Spirit, one of two things will happen to him. He will either pass out saying, 'These men are drunk', or he himself will be swept up by the fire into the Kingdom of God.'(23)

In the early days of the Salvation Army's 'Hallelujah Meetings' in the 1870s, people fell to the ground and there was weeping, shouting, clapping and dancing, visions and revelations. Unsure of what was happening, they called in doctors who took people out of the meetings!

Trance-like states have always been reported, often accompanied by visions. Wesley wrote about one woman affected by the revival in Everton. He asked her, 'Where have you been? She replied, 'I have been with my Saviour.' Wesley asked, 'In heaven or on earth?' 'I cannot tell, but I was in glory,' came the reply. (24)

Speaking in tongues

From the first-century upper room to the present day there has, on occasions, been speaking in tongues associated with outpourings of the Holy Spirit. It's not just a 20th century Pentecostal/Charismatic phenomena. Medieval mystics, Quakers, Anabaptists, and Methodists all had their tongues-speakers.

Thomas Walsh, one of Wesley's preachers wrote in 1750, 'This morning the Lord gave me language I knew not of, raising my soul to him in a wonderful manner.'(25) There was an outbreak of tongues in Scotland in the 1830s and at Edward Irving's church in Regent Square, London around the same time, which resulted in him being locked out of his own church.

Mrs Elizabeth Baxter was a reputable leader in the holiness and healing movement and cofounder of the Bethshan Healing Home in London. She told the International Conference of Holiness and Healing in 1885 that while in Germany, she preached for 35 minutes in German and was understood. Afterwards she often spoke to hundreds of people every day, yet outside the pulpit she did not understand or speak the language. (26)

During the Welsh revival there was apparently no speaking in tongues, but it has been recorded that young children began to speak in classic Welsh. (27)

An accompanying sign

However this gift was fully restored to the church during the Pentecostal revival of the early 1900s. It was seen as the sign that accompanied a true baptism in the Holy Spirit, and in the early days was misunderstood as a shortcut to language learning to help world evangelisation.

During the Pentecostal revival it was usual to testify about your experience to encourage others who were seeking the gift. Catherine Price, the first person to speak in tongues associated with this revival, wrote,

Who else was it but himself who filled my whole being with divine love, like fountains of warm oil springing up within, producing a spirit of unutterable adoration and praise to my blessed Lord...These languages were as avenues or doors by which I was led in and out of heaven. (28)

A revival of healing

The revival of holiness in the second half of the 19th century brought with it a revival of the ministry of healing. The reasoning was that if a person could be sanctified or cleansed from sin, then why should not their body, too, be rid of disease?

The 1880s were the 'Healing Decade' for Britain as this teaching became very popular. In London a healing home called Bethshan had been opened in 1865 by American holiness teacher W.E. Boardman, although the Quaker Elizabeth Baxter was its real founder and financial backer. She was a product of revival and edited a bi-monthly magazine called The Healer which publicised all the countless and remarkable healings that took place.

Brand new eyes

Here is one of the wonderful testimonies.

Five miles away lived George Evison. His eyeballs (in which disease commenced at five) fell out, both of them, within a few weeks, at about twenty. The poor, afflicted fellow was a curiosity. Hundreds gently placed their fingers in the empty eye sockets, little dreaming that they would thereby become later on witnesses to the 'healing.' Yet it was far more than a healing.

Hearing of the meetings, and having become a child of God during his affliction, he was conducted to the hall. After prayer and laying on of hands, a faint glimmer came. Within forty-eight hours new eyes, perfectly complete, but about the size of those of a boy of five, had been created by the Creator in those empty sockets. A considerable number of the public, doctors, solicitors, and other well-known people gave written testimony to the facts (Hebrews 13:8).

Through Mr. Evison's subsequent testimony, more than fifty received faith, and were healed of eye troubles or disease. The present writer knew his mother, and also many who knew him and who confirmed the fact. To him the mother related the incident, which the mother would be so sure of; his first eyes were blue grey, his new ones dark brown. Thus the Lord willed a double testimony. (29)

London in the 1880s

Other homes of faith and divine healing were opening in different parts of Britain where those needing healing could stay and receive teaching and prayer. Bethshan was well known. From it 'light and sound waves went round the world. Why? Christ was the centre and all radiation is from a centre.'(30)

In 1885 it hosted an International Conference on Holiness and Healing with 120 delegates including the radical Scottish healer, James Alexander Dowie who was later to found Zion City, Chicago. This healing camp was a root of Polly and Smith Wigglesworth's healing ministry. Polly was an associate of Elizabeth and was actually baptised by Dowie, and Smith's interest in healing was sparked in a Zion church in Leeds. Together they captured this healing revival in their spiritual DNA which was later to affect the world.

At Bethshan, miracles became such a usual occurrence that they were just accepted as a return to the Christianity of the early church. All this was happening in London in the 1880s. People expected signs and wonders to follow the preaching of the word, and they did.

The full gospel

The emphasis on healing in the Pentecostal revival was very important as part of the full gospel, Jesus – Sanctifier, Healer, Baptiser (in the Spirit) and Coming King. In Sunderland, the hub of the movement in Britain, many healings were recorded in the monthly paper, Confidence.

There was also teaching on the healing ministry especially that penned by Mary Boddy. People would travel to Sunderland to have her and her husband pray for them and a healing home was opened there for that very purpose. Integral to their message, they took Holiness teaching a stage further; healing was not just 'in the word' or 'in Christ' but also 'in the atonement.'

The Royal Touch

In this short excursus I am going to tell you about a practice of healing that doesn't fit into my normal grid! It's a little known fact that for over seven hundred years the monarchs of England (and France) held huge healing services wherever their court happened to be. The practice dated back to Edward the Confessor (11th century) who was reputed to have healing powers and ended in the reign of Queen Anne in 1712.

The monarch exercised the 'Royal Touch' (31) in formal healing services to cure scrofula, a form of tuberculosis which caused the sufferer to have boils all over his body. It was a common disease but it also served as a generic name for all skin diseases. In the ceremony the victim would kneel before the monarch and he would stroke the victim with both hands down his cheeks and throat whilst saying, 'The King toucheth thee; the Lord healeth thee.'

The practice reached a climax during the reign of Charles II who prayed for around 100,000 in his 25-year reign. Services were held several times a year and lasted up to three days with hundreds of ordinary people present. In one year alone in the 13th century Edward I blessed 1,760 people and testimonies of healings were recorded.

Francis MacNutt comments on this,

A wonderful thing is that the people – the ordinary people – were always looking for Jesus to heal them. For instance, when Charles I lost his battles...people still flocked to him to receive the Royal Touch as he travelled on his sorrowful way. So, when the healing ministry began to be revived, the people were still there waiting!

'These signs will follow those who believe...They will lay hands on the sick who will recover' – Mark 16:17-18. Not just kings or queens, not just saints, but those who believe. (32)

All of grace

For me this just illustrates the grace of God; that healing was an expression of God's mercy rather than the saintliness of the vessel he used. It was, of course, politically expedient for the monarchs to show they had a 'divine touch' to keep the general populace in awe of them.

We are royalty in the Kingdom and we can see this act as a prophetic sign of what God wants to do through us. He wants all Christians to exercise the 'royal touch' to see people healed and to touch the wounded and unlovely with the love of God.

Like those kings and queens of England all those years ago we can touch people with God's goodness. The Lord used immoral kings and queens because of grace. It's all of grace and we don't have to be ready or worthy, just available.

Places of pilgrimage

Where do we put relics, bones of saints, and places of pilgrimage where people claim to have been healed? Were these things just a point of contact with God where relationship had been denied?

John Wesley said he had always thought of these things as mere legend, as most Protestants do... After seeing miracles at the tomb of Abbe, Paris he commented, 'In many of those instances I see great superstition as well as strong faith. But the 'times of ignorance' does 'wink at' still; and bless the faith, notwithstanding the superstition.'(33)

Wonders in the heavens

During the Welsh Revival, Mary Jones lived in Egryn, a very small village on the west coast of Wales, when she began seeing 'wonders in the heaven above' (Acts 2:19), stars, pillars of fire and lights over houses. Having heard of the ministry of Evan Roberts, she had been praying for her friends, family and neighbours to be saved and these lights led her to those who needed Christ by hovering over their houses. Within two weeks, 51 became Christians as she was led to them.

On one occasion,

...she had seen the light hovering over some houses on the hilltop and was puzzled for she thought there was no one in those houses unconverted or at least out of church membership. But one day she was told...that there was one old woman in one of those houses now not on Christ's side. 'Ah that must be it,' she said. The two friends went up and found the woman, out of concern for her son. Mrs Jones visited her and she became one of the 51 in that marvellous fortnight. (34)

The Egryn Lights

The Egryn Lights, as they were called, were investigated by journalists from The Daily Mail and Mirror who clearly saw the lights.

A local journalist wrote,

...between us and the hills there suddenly flashed forth an enormously brilliant white light, and emitting from its whole circumference dazzling sparklets like flashing rays from a diamond...So far the light and the star had been equally visible to and seen alike by the five that formed our company.

Now it made a distinction...I suddenly saw three brilliant rays of dazzling white light stride across the road from mountain to sea throwing the stone wall into bold relief...as though a searchlight had been turned on that particular spot. There was not a living soul near, nor a house from which the light should have come.

Another short half mile and a blood-red light appeared to me in the centre of the village street just before us. I said nothing until we reached the spot. The red light disappeared as suddenly and mysteriously as it had come and there was absolutely nothing which could have been conceivable for it having been there before...These are simple facts, I offer no comment on them, I simply state what I saw.(35)

Mary saw them as lights that pointed to those who should be led to Christ, but Evan saw the lights as a sign and a wonder of a nation turning to God.

And more lights

Lights hovered over houses in the Hebrides Revival, and also lingered over All Saints Church one year before the Pentecostal revival began in Sunderland in 1907. Revd. A.A. Boddy saw it as a prophetic sign that blessings were going to radiate out from that place.

At the same time as the light appeared over the church roof, it also filled the room in the vicarage where he and three others were praying for revival. One of the men saw the Lord and suddenly fell to the floor crying, 'It's the Lord, there is no deception, brothers, it is the Lord himself.'(36)

Angels at Sunderland and beyond

Boddy had a real interest in angels, and during the revival several members of the congregation said they had seen them during the services. He was fascinated by stories of angels seen at the battle of Mons during August 1914 in the First World War and gathered together credible eye-witness reports. There are lengthy articles about it written by Boddy in several issues of Confidence.(37)

The witnesses said that at first three lights appeared in the sky and became brighter and their shapes could be seen, the middle angel having outstretched wings. One lengthy account by a soldier said that many were converted because of this. He couldn't understand how people back in Britain could laugh at the testimony of so many eye witnesses and say they were dreaming.

Signs on the earth below

Just prior to the First World War, evangelist Stephen Jeffries was preaching at Island Mission in Llanelly, South Wales just miles from Moriah Chapel, home of the Welsh Revival. It was an evening meeting and as he preached he became aware that the eyes of the congregation were fixed on the wall behind him. Turning around he saw the face of Jesus. At first it had been the head of a lamb, but then it gradually changed and became the face of the man of sorrows with a crown of thorns on his head.

The man of sorrows

In an interview for Confidence (38) Jeffries said, 'It was there for everyone to see, above the platform. It was a vision sent to us by the Lord. It reminded us that he was indeed the slain Lamb, and that that Lamb was identical with the crucified Saviour bearing the sin of the world. He seemed to be sorrowing with his people over the things which were coming upon the earth.'

Another eye witness said he went up to the wall; the vision was the size of a man's face and 'His eyes were remarkable, they seemed to be alive and moving.' Another commented, 'There was ineffable love and compassion shining out of his wonderful eyes.' It seemed that the face appeared out of a cloud.

The vision remained for six hours and the building was kept open. The interview continued, 'Many unbelievers came in and fell on their knees in penitence.' Next day the vision had disappeared.

Signs in their generation

Two men, both from humble beginnings, were raised up as signs to their generation. One English, one Welsh, they reached the peak of their ministries during the interwar years. Sometimes stories and testimonies in our history have that 'long ago and far away' feel about them but these men lived just outside the living memory period. They are Smith Wigglesworth and George Jeffries.

Smith Wigglesworth – apostle of faith

Wigglesworth (1859–1947) is a revival legend. His evangelistic healing ministry spanned forty years. He raised several from the dead, (39) cancers fell off people, blind eyes opened, limbs grew, those in wheelchairs got up and ran...the stories seem to go on and on.

Thousands would pack halls wherever he went. At the beginning of meetings he would announce that the first person to stand, whatever the ailment, would be healed. And so they were. Called 'the apostle of faith,' he would say, 'I am not moved by what I see or hear. I am moved by what I believe.'(40)

Evangelism was his heartbeat. In one sermon he said, 'I am out to win people for Jesus. It's my business to win souls. It's my business to make everyone hungry, dissatisfied. It is my business to make people either glad or mad. I have a message from heaven and that will not leave people as I find them.'(41)

Signs followed the man

In the early days he visited a Mrs Clark who was dying at home. Not knowing any better, he poured half a pint of oil over her. Jesus appeared at the foot of the bed and smiled. In later years, he said that he never forgot that beautiful, soft smile. It was a day that changed his life as strength entered the lady and she lived many more years totally well.(42)

From 1889 he led Bowland Street Mission in Bradford, Yorkshire with his wife Polly. Even before his baptism in the Holy Spirit they were seeing regular healings. After this encounter, a new power entered him and he travelled round the country with Polly. Wherever they went, people were filled with the Holy Spirit and healed until the sad day in 1914 when his beloved wife died. Following this, the anointing on him grew stronger. He travelled the world and in 1922 took Australia and New Zealand by storm as he carried revival there.

One more story... Matthew was a boy with a heart condition, whose body had become like a skeleton. Wigglesworth told the parents to air his clothes and put his socks on. He went and laid hands on him and the glory was so strong in the room that Wigglesworth fell face down on the floor. The whole room including the bed shook. Matthew got up and dressed. The same glory filled the kitchen and his parents fell down. Matthew's sister was healed from a mental condition. In fact, revival came to that village. (43)

I move the Spirit

Audacious, bold, blunt, unique are words that could be used to describe Wigglesworth. His methods were controversial but his somewhat gruff exterior housed a heart of compassion. His spiritual secret was reliance on the Spirit of God and confidence in the word of God. (44) He famously once said, 'If the Spirit does not move me, I move the Spirit...as I start out in the natural, in faith, the Spirit of God always meets me and anoints me.'(45)

George Jeffries – a child of revival

Following the Welsh revival, George (1887-1962) and Stephen Jeffries

(1876-1943) were part of a group who wanted to see the same revival power again. They called themselves 'children of the revival.' Stephen, in whose meeting was the vision of Christ's face, became a pastor in Llanelli while George went on to become one of the most successful healing evangelists this country has ever known.

After some time in Ireland where he formed the Elim Evangelistic Band, George returned to England in 1921. His crusades filled the largest halls in the land with thousands converted and healed. The news was carried by the national press.

In his book, Healing Rays, there are photographs of halls where he preached crammed full with people.(46) Between 1926 and 1939 he filled the Royal Albert Hall in London fifty times and at Easter time he would hold mass baptisms there. One Whitsun at the Albert Hall, 300 were filled with the Holy Spirit at the same time and spoke in tongues.

Between 1930 and 1936 he filled the Crystal Palace, London seven times before it was burnt down. At that time it was the largest exhibition centre in the world. His 1930 campaign in Bingley Hall, the largest hall in Birmingham, saw 10,000 converts. One thousand were miraculously healed and 1,100 baptised.

The interwar years were the golden years of Pentecostalism. Scores of Elim churches were planted in the wake of his crusades, 133 churches by 1933.(47) Like the initial Pentecostal revival that was stopped in its tracks by the First World War, this new thrust of revival fervour came to an end as the Second World War began in 1939.(48)

The acts of the apostles

Jeffries' was a supernatural ministry. Wherever he went with his revival party they prayed for the sick. His book, Healing Rays is full of testimonies and reads like a continuation of the Acts of the Apostles. He wrote,

Throughout our land today there are multitudes who testify before wondering congregations of their deliverances from all kinds of physical ailments.

Cripples have stepped out of wheelchairs and carriages and are now walking as other people. The paralysed and lame have discarded their crutches and are confirming their testimony by walking unaided. Eyes once wrapped in the blackness and darkness of midnight now see the light of glorious day. Deaf ears, shut in with strange and unnatural silence, now respond to sweet music and the singing of the birds. Bodies weary and worn by various diseases have been quickened, relieved and delivered. The oppressed crushed by ever-increasing burdens have been uplifted and raised.

Thus the testimonies go forth while manifested healings and miracles confirm. The happenings of today are akin to those we read of in the Bible. The healings of today are exactly like those of the days of the apostles. (49)

Two healing testimonies
These are just two of the stories he relates.

Florence Munday of Southampton had been in a wheelchair with tuberculosis for fourteen years and also had a skin disease. She was in great pain and was told her leg had to be amputated. She was anointed with oil and after prayer testified that her body 'vibrated with life.' Her leg grew four and a half inches and she got out of the wheelchair completely healed. She was the first to be baptised at the Albert Hall meeting of 1938. (50)

James Gregson from Leeds was healed in 1927. He could only walk on crutches and dragged his legs behind him. When Jeffries laid his hands on him he said it felt like a dozen hands were placed all over his body, and every bone went back into place. He was instantly healed as well as saved. In two weeks he had gained two stone, five pounds and was able to go back to work.(51)

Yesterday, today and forever
How I'd love to tell more stories ... like in Wigglesworth's meetings the deaf heard, the blind saw, cancers disappeared and discarded wheelchairs, braces and crutches told their own story. In fact many had been stored in the basement of London's Kensington Temple where Jeffries ministered powerfully and were discovered in the 1960s. (52) Jeffries believed that revival is always available because the Holy Spirit is always moving. And because Jesus is the same 'yesterday, and today and for ever' (Hebrews 13:8), that same power available to him is available to us.(53)

Only believe

Signs from heaven will always make us wonder in amazement, just as they have done throughout our history for those who have ears to hear and eyes to see. I finish this chapter with the words of an old chorus that was a favourite of the 'apostle of faith,' based on the words of Jesus in Mark 9:23, 'Everything is possible for him who believes.'

'Only believe, only believe,
All things are possible, only believe.'

Endnotes

1. Bede, *The Ecclesiastical History of the English People*, Oxford University Press, Oxford, UK, 2008, p 58.

2. A.J. Gordon, *The Ministry of Healing*, Fleming H. Revel Co., New York, USA, 1882, e text www.revival-library.org, p 16.

3. Roberts Liardon, *God's Generals, The Roaring Reformers*, Whitaker House, New Kensington, USA, 2003, p 357.

4. Ibid., p 351.

5. Jeff Doles, *Miracles and Manifestations of the Holy Spirit in the History of the Church*, Walking Barefoot Ministries, Florida, USA, 2008, p 190. A quote from Edmund Goerke, *The Gift of Healing in the Life of George Fox*, www.quakerinfo.com/healing1.shtml.

6. Ibid., p 189. A quote from Fox's Journal, Chapter 18.

7. Doles, ibid., p 208. A quote from John Wesley's Journal, March 17th 1746.

8. Ibid., December 25th 1742.

9. A Skevington Wood, *The Burning Heart*, Cliff College Publishing, Sheffield, U.K., 2001, p177.

10. Doles, op.cit., p 201. John Wesley's Journal, April 1739.

11. Patrick Dixon, *Signs of Revival*, Kingsway, Eastbourne, UK, 1994, p 136.

12. Doles, op.cit., pp 212-3. John Wesley's Journal, May 30th 1759.

13. Doles, op.cit., p 215. November 24th 1759 *Works of John Wesley, History of the Methodists*.

14. Doles, op.cit., p 214. John Wesley's Journal, May 30th 1759.

15. Doles, op.cit., John Wesley's Journal, July 6-7th 1739.

16. Doles, op.cit., p 219. *Works of John Wesley, Vol. 7*, Sermon no. 89, 'The More Excellent Way.'

17. George Jeffries, *Healing Rays*, first published 1932, p 121. www.revival-library.org

18. A.J. Gordon, op.cit., p 44.

19. Jeffries, op.cit., p 125.

20. Duncan Campbell, *When the Mountains Flowed Down*, a transcribed message, www.revival-library.org/catalogues/20thcenttury/campbell.html

21. Dixon, Patrick, op.cit., p 125. John Wesley's Journal, May 9th 1740.

22. Dixon, op.cit., p 155.

23. Dixon, op.cit., p 169.

24. Dixon, op.cit., p 138.

25. Dixon, op.cit., p 133.

26. Nathaniel Wiseman, Elizabeth Baxter, The Christian Herald Co., London, UK, 1928 p 67-8, digital book www.revival-library.org

27. J. Edwin Orr, *The Flaming Tongue*, Moody Press, Chicago, USA, 1973, p 21.

28. Stanley Frodsham, *With Signs Following*, Gospel Publishing House, Springfield, USA, 1946, pp 67,70 digital book www.revival-library.org

29. Wiseman, op.cit., pp 227-8.

30. Wiseman, op.cit., p 227.

31. See Marc Bloch, *The Royal Touch*, Dorset Press, New York, USA, 1961.

32. Francis MacNutt, *The Royal Touch*, (article) www.christianhealingministries.org/newsletter/1993/htm. See also Francis MacNutt, *The Nearly Perfect Crime*, Chosen, Grand Rapids, USA, pp 133-137.

33. Doles, op.cit., p 211. John Wesley's Journal, January 11th 1750.

34. Karen Lowe, *Carriers of the Fire*, Shedhead Productions, Llanelli, UK, 2004, p 113.

35. Ibid., p114.

36. William K. Kay, William, *Inside Story*, Mattersey Hall Publishing, Mattersey, UK, 1990, p 21.

37. *Confidence* March 1916, p 48, September 1915, pp 164-67, www.revival-library.org.

38. *Confidence* September 1915, pp 164-5.

39. Actual numbers vary according to the sources; 14 is a number that reoccurs!

40. Stanley Frodsham, *Apostle of Faith*, Gospel Publishing House, Springfield, USA, 1993, p 68.

41. Philip Taylor, *In the Steps of Smith Wigglesworth*, Philip B. Taylor (pub), 2007, p 38.

42. Frodsham, *Apostle*, op.cit., p 36.

43. Ibid., pp 50-1.

44. Ibid., p 109.

45. Ibid., p 128.

46. Jeffries, op.cit., pp 156-7.

47. Roberts Liardon, *God's Generals: The Healing Evangelists*, Whitaker House, New Kensington, USA, 2011, p 68.

48. Ibid., pp 72-88, a discussion of other reasons.

49. Jeffries, op.cit., pp 58-9.

50. Jeffries, op.cit., pp 178-80.

51. Jeffries, op.cit., pp 180-1.

52. Liardon, *Healing Evangelists*, op.cit., p 89.

53. Ibid., p 73.

7
The Breath of Heaven

'Only God can make a community God-conscious. Just think about what would happen if God came to any community in power. I believe that day is coming.' Duncan Campbell

Heaven meets earth

The Celts called them 'thin places,' where the distinction between heaven and earth was blurred as they lived with a conscious awareness of another world. 'They found a swamp, a moor, a thicket, a rock, and they made an Eden in the wilderness' (1) in a deliberate attempt to create the environment of heaven. In the same way, the Puritans who went to New England set about cultivating the same garden paradise. (2)

The men of the Old Testament built altars after encountering the divine, as permanent markers of where heaven touched earth. Can you imagine the atmosphere of heaven that Jesus carried around with him? There were breakouts of miracles wherever he went because there is complete wholeness in heaven.

One eye-witness said about the revival in the Hebrides, 'You are brought in touch with the power of the world to come and something indefinable lives within you. You can never be content with anything less than you have seen; and you live to see it again.' Another commented, 'We still feel we are a waiting community, waiting for the breath from heaven.'

Outbreak!

In the second chapter of the book of Acts we read what happened when heaven descended into the upper room on 120 disciples:

Suddenly a sound like the blowing of a violent wind came from heaven and filled the whole house where they were sitting. They saw what seemed to be tongues of fire that separated and come to rest on each of them. All of them were filled with the Holy Spirit and began to speak in other tongues as the Spirit enabled them.

It was 9 o'clock in the morning, and I wonder what they had been doing prior to this heavenly outbreak: talking together, resting, praying or even eating breakfast. Whatever it was, there was certainly a dramatic shift in the atmosphere. The disciples were never the same again, as they carried the atmosphere of the upper room beyond the confines of closed doors.

Heaven filled the city

Overcome by their experience and behaving like drunk men and women, they took heaven onto the streets of Jerusalem. Masses of people gathered around, drawn not just by their unusual behaviour, but by the presence of God that lingered around them. We read that the crowds were 'amazed and perplexed,' asking in today's language, 'What on earth is going on?'

The breath of heaven was not just in the disciples, but around them, and the atmosphere changed wherever they went in the city. Soon all Jerusalem was filled with their teaching, yes, but also with the presence of God. Sick people lying on beds and mats were brought out of their houses by family and friends to line the streets, hoping that Peter's shadow might fall on them and they would be healed. Crowds were drawn from the towns around bringing the sick and all of them were healed too (Acts 5:15-16, 28).

On the first day of heaven's breakout, 3,000 accepted the message and were baptised. Every day more and more men and women were saved and joined this first group of believers (Acts 2:41, 47).

A community saturated with God

How I would have loved to have visited the Hebridean Islands of Lewis and Harris during the years 1949-52! Many who did became vividly conscious of the spiritual atmosphere before they reached the island. It's an inspirational example of what can happen when the breath of heaven blows through a community.

Duncan Campbell, the man used by God at this time, wrote about 'a community saturated with God.' He refers to a 'revival,' but I think the term 'awakening' better describes what happened.

First, let me tell you what I mean by revival. An evangelistic campaign or special meeting is not revival. In a successful evangelistic campaign or crusade, there will be hundreds or even thousands of people making decisions for Jesus Christ, but the community remains untouched, and the churches continue much the same as before the outreach.

In revival, God moves in the district. Suddenly, the community becomes God-conscious. The Spirit of God grips men and women in such a way that even work is given up as people give themselves to waiting upon God. In the midst of the Lewis awakening, the parish minister at Barvas wrote, 'The Spirit of the Lord was resting wonderfully on the different townships of the region. His presence was in the homes of the people, on meadow and moorland, and even on the public roads...'

Campbell continued,

It takes the supernatural to break the bonds of the natural. You can make a community mission-conscious. You can make a community crusade-conscious. But only God can make a community God-conscious. Just think about what would happen if God came to any community in power. I believe that day is coming. May God prepare us all for it. Amen. (3)

Amen indeed.

Hunger gripped the people

There was such a spontaneity associated with this move of the Holy Spirit. As Campbell said, 'A hunger gripped the people.' The first night he spoke at Barvas. As he opened the doors to leave the church following the close of the meeting at 11.00pm, 600 men and women stood in the churchyard having been drawn there by the Holy Spirit.

Some who had gone to bed got up again and dressed, and in the parish hall the power of God fell on over 100 young people at a dance and they ran to the church.

At four in the morning Campbell was at last on his way home when he was asked to go to the police station. Four hundred had gathered, convicted of their sins and even as he walked there he saw men were on their knees by the roadside.

In another village called Arnol, Campbell had been holding a few meetings, but because the response had not been great, some believers were holding a prayer meeting in their home at the end of an evening. They became aware among them that their prayers had been heard and so they finished praying and left the house only to find other villagers walking towards the church where Campbell still was, drawn from their houses by the Holy Spirit. They were carrying chairs, in case there was no room in the church, as the whole community was swept by the Spirit of God.

Loosing heaven

Little Donald was powerfully baptised in the Holy Spirit. As he prayed aloud in a prayer meeting in his church, he saw into heaven and pulled down what he saw: 'God, there is power there, let it loose!' The power fell and half the people slumped on top of each other 'like corn before a sickle.' Others fell into a trance with hands held high and remained that way for over two hours.

What happened next is remarkable. Men of the same clan who were out in their boats fishing felt the power and made for the shore and on to the church. One schoolmaster on the mainland, again of the same clan, left his house at 10:00 at night, drove 15 miles and took the ferry to the island and made his way to the church.

One of the 'affected' families in the church had a daughter living in London. At the same time as this was all going on she was walking along Oxford Street and was hit by the power of God.

Talking about the Hebrides in the mid 20th century, Campbell said, 'The presence of God was a universal, inescapable fact; at home, in the church, and by the roadside.'(4)

There's something in me that cries out, 'Lord, do it again in our day and generation!'

Drawn by the presence

In the Hebrides people were drawn irresistibly by the Holy Spirit to places where they could meet with God in a corporate way. Many just encountered God at the roadside or at home, but this drawing was a phenomena which reminds me of the gentle pull that we read of in Hosea, where God draws his people with cords of love and kindness (Hosea 11:4).

In the 1859 revival that started in Coleraine, Northern Ireland there's a remarkable story that involved some schoolboys. One boy shouted out in the school room, 'I am so happy! I have the Lord Jesus in my heart.' These words carried such an anointing that one after the other boys left the class and knelt down alongside a wall in the playground.

Soon the whole school was on its knees and the prayers could be heard outside in the streets. People were drawn into the school out of more than curiosity, and began crying out to God like the boys until they filled every room as the Holy Spirit descended on them.(5)

An extraordinary, ordinary home

Catherine Price was the first person in Britain to be baptised in the Holy Spirit and speak in tongues in association with the 20th century Pentecostal revival. She was married to a bank manager in London in 1907. Several months before the outpouring in Sunderland, the little prayer meetings she held at her home became places of heaven on earth. Because of the presence of God people sought out her terraced house in an ordinary street until her two rooms were overflowing and people had to sit on the stairs.

Her words captured something of what it was like.

A few of us who met for prayer at the beginning will never forget the awe of God's holy presence, as the room and everything in it gently rocked... All who were ailing and sick in that meeting testified afterwards that God's love as a burning stream healed them. No man touched them or even prayed for them. Another time his presence was as a wind and we were as mown grass before him. (6) Such it is when the breath of heaven comes.

Glory dwells in the land

The great 20th century preacher, C.H. Spurgeon, commented on these verses from Psalm 85:9 (KJV) in relation to the Second Evangelical Awakening, *'Surely his salvation is nigh them that fear him; that glory may dwell in our land.'* He wrote,

By his coming, salvation is brought near, and glory, even the glory of the presence of the Lord, tabernacles among men... Revival has an atmosphere that can be felt; and the presence of God comes down [which is] very real and glory dwells in the land. (7)

That's what happened in the fishing port of Lowestoft, on the East Anglian coast in 1921. During that summer under the preaching of Douglas Brown they had 'known the felt presence of Christ' not just in the town but all around East Anglia. (8)

An awakening had come to the community. One morning a man could be seen pacing up and down outside Douglas Brown's hotel while he was having breakfast. Others were kneeling on the pavement or hanging over railings by the harbour praying. Churches were overflowing and in the streets and along footpaths kneeling figures could be seen, as one after the other encountered the atmosphere of heaven.

Carrying the presence

Another man God used in this awakening was the Scotsman, Jock Troup. When Jock preached in Great Yarmouth, another fishing port not far from Lowestoft, men were saved out at sea, miles out of earshot of the preaching!

God came down into the market place after the stalls had closed and strong fishermen fell to the ground under conviction of sin, while others knelt in the street in the rain. Fisher girls were similarly affected and unable to work in the curing yards until they were right with God. (9)

When Jock left for Fraserburgh in North East Scotland, the powerful presence of God went with him. Once the herring season came to an end and the Scottish fishermen and women returned to their home ports, they too carried the same heavy presence with them and it blanketed the east coast.

Changed communities

It was noted in the 1921 East Anglian awakening, 'Among the 10,000 inhabitants of Lowestoft, drunkenness declined, the police had fewer people to deal with from the dens of vice in the town and former blasphemers became men of prayer.' 'Revival calmed the social unrest because of economic depression, high unemployment.'(10) This has always been the case wherever the breath of heaven has blown through a community.

In the Hebrides, 'Drinking houses closed permanently and dance halls closed because all the young people were at the prayer meetings.'(11)

In a revival that swept Kilsyth, Scotland in 1839, 'The public houses, the coal pits, the harvest-reaping fields, the weaving loomsteads, the recesses of our glens...all may be called to witness that there is a mighty change in our place for the better' and 'the voice of prayer and praise almost in every house.'(12)

During the 1859 revival in Scotland one minister wrote, 'There is a visible change in the town; there is a restraint of evil...I never expected to see so much of heaven this side of time'. (13)

Way back when Puritan Richard Baxter was a minister in Kidderminster in the 1600s, it's said that on Sundays 'the streets were quiet, there was no disorder and all you could hear were a hundred families singing psalms in their homes.'(14)

An irresistible cleansing ozone

Speaking in 1749 John Wesley said,

A few years ago Great Britain and Ireland were covered with vice from sea to sea. Very little of even the form of religion was left, and still less of the power of it. Out of this darkness God commanded light to shine...

The habitual drunkard that was is now temperate in all things; the whoremonger now flees fornication; he that stole, steals no more, but works with his hands; he that cursed or swore, perhaps at every sentence, has now learned to serve the Lord...those formally enslaved to various habits of sin are now brought to...habits of holiness. These are demonstrable facts. (15)

150 years later one historian wrote regarding Britain, 'Wesley swept the dead air with irresistible, cleansing ozone. To thousands of men and women his preaching and gospel revealed a new heaven and a new earth.'(16)

White gloves in Wales

The social impact of the 1904 Welsh revival was remarkable. In some communities the magistrates were presented with white gloves because there were no cases to try. The policeman found themselves unemployed and so they formed choirs to sing in the chapels. As one person remarked, 'The community had been converted into a praying multitude.'(17)

The area most affected by the revival was the coal mining valleys of South Wales. The lives of the miners were transformed. Instead of going straight from the pit head to the taverns, the men went to the chapels.

Down the mines there were impromptu prayer meetings and as a newfound gentleness swept over the men, it affected their speech. The pit ponies had been used to harsh language and now they stood confused as the miners spoke softly to them until they got used to their new way of talking.

One touching thing that happened was that many families who had put their elderly parents into the workhouse, those inhuman institutions which still were around even in the 20th century, fetched them out to look after them themselves.

A London journalist writing about the revival noted that certainly many drinking places that had been crowded were empty, the frequenters being led away either by the religious workers in person... or by the *irresistible spirit of the movement*. One man commented, 'Aye, there's something funny about it. They say you feel it as soon as you are inside the building where he's [Evan Roberts] going to speak.'(18)

The same sorts of things happened in the revival of 1859. One local policeman was reprimanded by his chief constable for attending the prayer meetings and defended himself by saying that the roads were quiet, the taverns were empty and the chapels were the only places of excitement!(19)

She carried heaven

A revivalist who carried heaven with her was Phoebe Palmer. As she made her way around Britain in the years between 1859-63, towns were transformed. In Cardiff because of 'a remarkable work of the Spirit,' a detective said that 'Cardiff had become a different place.'(20)

The Palmers originally intended to stay in Sunderland for two weeks but stayed for 35 days as the whole community of 100,000 was dramatically affected. Crime was greatly reduced and magistrates were given white gloves just as in Wales. The local press commented that if things continued, there might have to be a reduction of the police force.(21)

So full of God

These three stories tell us what it must have been like to come into contact with Smith Wigglesworth. He was a man who was so full of God that the atmosphere around him must have carried God's kindness, since it's the kindness of God that leads people to repentance (Romans 2:4).

One day Smith was in a railway carriage which was full of people but he hadn't spoken to them. After a while he left to wash his hands and when he came back one man jumped up and said, 'Sir, you convince me of sin,' and fell on his knees. Then the whole carriage of people cried out in the same way. They said, 'Who are you? What are you? You convince us all of sin,' and Smith led them to the Lord. (22)

Smith said, 'Wherever I went conviction seemed to be upon people.' Another story was when he walked into a grocer's shop and three people fell to their knees in repentance. Another time there were two ladies working in a field as Smith passed by. He called out, 'Are you saved?' and the ladies dropped their buckets immediately and called out for salvation.(23)

Carrying the fire

Smith travelled to Sunderland because he heard that people there were being baptised in the Holy Spirit and were speaking in tongues and this is what he wanted too. He was hungry and the power of the Spirit filled the man.

A characteristic of the Pentecostal revival was that it was highly transferable. Following Smith's visit to Sunderland where he was baptised in the Holy Spirit and spoke with tongues, he carried that anointing back to the Bowland Street Mission in Bradford. The new power and authority that accompanied his words was evident. After he preached, one man stood up and said he wanted what Smith had, and that's when the congregation found themselves on the floor laughing with 'holy laughter.' Following this, many more in Bradford were baptised in the Spirit.

Wherever Smith and Polly went and ministered, people experienced the same baptism, maybe not always the laughter, but certainly the power and speaking in tongues. But this is just what happened to so many men and women who went to Sunderland; they caught the fire and set their own towns ablaze.

Association and impartation

It was through association as well as impartation that the Pentecostal revival spread. It's as we encounter spiritual atmospheres that we are changed. When Saul met the company of prophets at Gibeah he was changed into a different person and began prophesying with them. He had encountered a different atmosphere which was resident in those prophets and together they created a corporate prophetic environment (1 Samuel 10:5-12).

I'm sure this has happened many times in our history. At Wesley and Whitefield's huge gatherings, even if some at the back could not hear what they were saying, they must have encountered the atmosphere of heaven these men created with their words as its influence spread out over the fields.

Intentional journeys to places where the Spirit of God is moving, chance meetings, being in the company of those fresh from heavenly encounters, as well as times when the glory of God descends sovereignly on a community, all bring us in contact with the breath of heaven. When that happens, we can't remain the same.

Valuing the presence

In Exodus 33:15 we are told that Moses so valued the presence of God that he didn't want to move from the place he was unless the presence of God went with him. He entreated the Lord, 'show me your glory,' and God responded by passing in front of him with his goodness.

It's this goodness that got down deep into the lives of those transformed by these awakenings and revivals, which in turn transformed their communities. People no longer gained any pleasure from sin but inherent in the glory that fell was heaven's goodness. In the next chapter we'll see how these encounters with goodness propelled men and women to 'do good' in their Jerusalem and to the ends of the earth.

Living in the upper room

I don't believe that we have to wait to encounter the atmosphere of heaven. We have a standing invitation to go through the open door (Revelation 4:1) into a realm of heavenly reality. As we do, the breezes of heaven will sweep over us, filling our lungs so we can be carriers of another world and bring heaven to earth.

The upper room experience of the disciples can be experienced again and again and like the 120 we can fill our towns and cities with the breath of heaven as we become carriers of his presence.

Awake, north wind, and come, south wind!
Blow on my garden, that its fragrance may spread abroad.
Song of Songs 4:16

Endnotes

1. David J. Bosch, *Transforming Mission*, Orbis, New York, 1998, p 232.
2. Ibid., p 300.
3. Duncan Campbell, *When the Mountains Flowed Down*, a transcribed message, www.revival-library.org/catalogues/20thcenttury/campbell.html
4. Ibid.
5. Arthur Wallis, *In the Day of Your Power*, Christian Literature Crusade, Alresford, UK, 1989, pp 68-8.
6. Stanley Frodsham, *With Signs Following*, Gospel Publishing House, Springfield, USA, 1946, p 72. www.revival-library.org
7. Stanley Griffin, *A Forgotten Revival*, Day One Publications, Bromley, UK, 1992, p 106.
8. Ibid., p 108.
9. Ibid., p 108.
10. Ibid., p 100.
11. Campbell, op.cit.

12. Wallis, op.cit., p 72.

13. Wallis, op.cit., p 73.

14. William Allen, *The History of Revivals of Religion*, Revival Publishing Company, Co. Antrim, UK, 1951, p 21.

15. A. Skevington Wood, *The Burning Heart*, Cliff College Publishing, Sheffield, 2001, p 179.

16. Ibid., quoting C. Grant Robinson.

17. J. Edwin Orr, *Flaming Tongue*, Moody Press, Chicago, USA, 1973, p 11.

18. Patrick Dixon, *Signs of Revival*, Kingsway, Eastbourne, UK, 1994, p 165.

19. J. Edwin Orr, *The Second Evangelical Awakening in Britain*, Marshall, Morgan and Scott, London; Edinburgh, UK, 1949, p 86.

20. Ibid., p 91.

21. *The Northern Daily Express*, November 1859.

22. Stanley Frodsham, *Apostle of Faith*, Gospel Publishing House, Springfield, USA, 1993, p 80.

23. Ibid., pp 48-49.

8
Home and Away

By their fruit you will recognise them.
Matthew 7:20

No branch can bear fruit by itself; it must remain in the vine.
John 15:4

The best they could

Whether it be the first or twenty-first century, those whose hearts, like Wesley's, have been 'strangely warmed' have had birthed within them a desire to spread the gospel, the good news. How that has found expression has been different in each succeeding generation. It's so easy for us to look back with a critical spirit at men and women who sought as best they knew how to do the best they could with the light they had.

So right at the beginning of this chapter I want to acknowledge that, yes, there have been gross misuses of power in the name of Christ both at home and away. Mission's darkest hour was during the crusades of the 11th–13th centuries.

In addition, with 21st century hindsight, we would all agree that there was often an unholy mixture of gospel and western culture as Britain extended her Empire. Instead of signs and wonders there have been 'signs and blunders.'(1)

Nevertheless, Christ has been preached in word and deed, and that is a reason to be glad (Philippians 1:15-18).

Celebrate the good

I fully understand the concern about this darker side. Let's learn from it so we don't repeat our mistakes, and let's repent where it is needed. But what I want to do is celebrate the good, and there has been a lot!

This little island in the north of the world would fit scores of times into some of the larger nations. Its location could have made it isolated and inconsequential in world history, but it has been a major player on the world stage. Why should English be the most widely spoken language across our world?

God has visited us time and time again. At home much of our social transformation came about as an expression of love for God and our fellow man, while this same love propelled thousands of men and women to the ends of the earth to take the gospel to the nations. We have made a difference. That's not to make us proud, but in humility to acknowledge God's divine grace and favour on 90,000 or so square miles of land and its inhabitants in the middle of the North Sea.

A rich soil

There have always been individual Christians who have stood head and shoulders above the rest in their sacrificial care for humanity, but in times of revival the numbers are multiplied. When the breath of heaven descends, lives are transformed and hearts begin to beat with God's heart for his world. Some recognised poverty and all manner of social evils on their doorstep and did something about it. Others were gripped with God's heart for the nations and went.

It is one thing to be moved to love your brother, to engage in good works or take a boat to China in the first flush of salvation, but we are in this for the long haul. What happens after the waves of revival recede or the heavy presence lifts is a mark of the ongoing transformation it has brought to individual lives, communities and the nation as a whole. In Britain we have rich soil to explore and so much of the good fruit remains.

The first social services

As Christians in this nation we are a result of cross-cultural mission, from the Roman invaders of the first century, to Augustine and his band of continental monks in the sixth. Meanwhile, Celtic monks from the fringes of this island travelled through Britain's internal kingdoms establishing communities of believers. Britain was evangelised.

The monastic system developed separately from the church as an institution. Throughout the Middle Ages these working monasteries provided the first social services, extending the love of Christ by feeding the hungry, looking after the sick and distributing their herbal medicines. They were places of rest for travellers and also provided education for boys. They were centres of culture as well as mission.

Living in Christendom

All the while churches were built in the towns and surrounding villages, and Britain's parish system began to take shape. Everyone knew their place in society and understood that salvation was to be found in the church. To be born in this country meant you lived in Christendom. Mission or reform was deemed unnecessary and the church's main task was to shield the common people from evil and heresy, which were seen as subversive to the status quo.

By and large the established church had become thoroughly institutionalised. The notion of Christendom remained even after the Reformation, and still lingers today. Many people write Church of England as their religion on official forms, even though they may never set foot in a church.

The winds begin to blow

It wasn't until fresh winds of the Spirit began to blow over the pages of the newly translated Word of God in English that revelation came, understanding quickened and social reform and mission as we know it was born.

The Puritans grappled with the idea of what it meant for the kingdom of God to come on earth, and concluded that England needed to be transformed into a theocracy for that to happen. However, I for one would not have wanted to live in Cromwell's England!

But the Quakers, as they heard God's voice, spoke and acted prophetically. The internal freedom that the Holy Spirit brought enabled them to stand against the established social order, and that's why they got into so much trouble with the authorities. Undeterred, their devotion to Christ found outward expression in many humanitarian reforms and mission. Their impact was enormous and we live in the good of it even today, 400 years later.

Born out of theology

What we believe really does affect what we do, and the Quakers' 'inner light' principle caused them to have a high regard for all humanity. Their egalitarian message not only saw the potential in every man and woman to respond to the gospel, but also gave them equal respect and honour. This was certainly not universally the case in Britain at that time.

Active reformers

Quakers were the first to take a stand against slavery. As early as 1657, Fox wrote to Friends in the colonies who were slave owners, reminding them that God is no respecter of persons. He encouraged them to teach the slaves skills, and then free them. Many were active in anti-slavery societies across Britain and instrumental in its abolition. It was Quakers who presented the first anti-slavery petition to Parliament in 1783 and supported the subsequent Acts of Parliament banning slavery and the slave trade.

Elizabeth Fry (1780-1845) was a Quaker minister who campaigned for prison reform resulting in the 1823 Gaols Act. In 1835 she was even invited to speak in the House of Lords when she told her audience that it was only the truths of the Bible that could change a human heart.

Quaker women were active in suffrage unions and a fiery campaigner, Ann Knight, wrote the first leaflet on women's suffrage in 1847. She even had a village in Jamaica, Knightsville, named after her following an anti-slavery campaign. Quakers also pioneered education for both girls and boys, as well as higher education. In fact, their reform activities seem endless.

When you eat a bar of Cadbury's chocolate or a Huntley and Palmer's biscuit while drinking a cup of tea from a Wedgwood cup (unlikely, I know!), remind yourself that the founders of these companies were all Quakers who believed in social welfare and the educational development of their workers. An area of Birmingham called Bourneville where houses are laid out around a park stands as a testimony to Mr. Cadbury.

Far-flung missions

From Turkey to the American colonies, Quaker men and women fearlessly preached the gospel. At a time when women had a prescribed role, the freedom of Quaker women was astounding, even more so when you read their stories. One lady, Mary Fisher, preached to the Sultan of Turkey who asked her to stay in the country, since he couldn't help but respect someone who had travelled so far with a message from the Lord.

In the colonies

Later Mary preached in the American colonies, but her life ended there as she was marched through the streets to the sound of drums to her place of execution by hanging. The Puritans who had left Britain for religious freedom were repeating the same persecution they had experienced. But still the Quakers came with their message.

Fox himself travelled to the West Indies and spent two years in New England where he loved preaching to the Native Americans. Another Quaker, William Penn, was given land by Charles II to set up a colony in America solely for Quakers who wanted religious freedom, which is the story behind Pennsylvania.

Fox and the Friends were certainly the forerunners of mission and social reform.

The reward of his suffering

It was the Moravians who really started the ball rolling in terms of modern missions. Their passionate rallying cry was, 'May the Lamb that was slain receive the reward of his suffering.' Their goal was the salvation of as many souls as possible. They went to great lengths travelling to remote parts of the world to achieve this, and while on their way ministered to the poor, sick and destitute.

The Moravians were a huge influence on the young John Wesley as he spent time with them before embarking on the ministry that changed the face of Britain.

A social reformer

Like the Moravians, Wesley's main focus was the salvation of souls. However, he looked to the renewing of the nation as inner transformation of hearts found expression in good works.

He famously said, 'Do all the good you can, by all the means you can, in all the ways you can, in all the places you can, at all the times you can, to all the people you can, as long as ever you can.' (2) That's what Wesley was about!

Britain was a dangerous place to be in the 18th century. Highwaymen held up stagecoaches on the roads, life in the towns and cities was marked by drunkenness, immorality and corruption and the common people lived a hand-to-mouth existence.

Wesley was known to say, 'I bear the rich and love the poor'(3) and he spent most of his time with the latter. The mining areas of Kingswood, Bristol were his favourite places for preaching.

Although his passion was the salvation of souls, Wesley found time to start dispensaries for the sick and helped the poor to help themselves with relief and benefit societies.(4) He set up schools and orphanages and wrote books to teach reading. He exposed the need for reforms in prisons and workhouses, and the last letter he wrote was to Wilberforce, encouraging him in his campaign to end slavery.

The world was their parish

Wesley, Whitefield and other Methodist preachers were committed to world evangelisation. The world, rather than the confines of Christendom was their parish.(5) During Wesley's life time there was no particular Methodist sending strategy but Whitefield led the way in the evangelisation of America through the American First Great Awakening of the mid-1700s.

The Methodist patron, the Countess of Huntington, had a remarkable missionary vision for a woman of her time. In 1792 she began connexion chapels for freed slaves in Freetown, Sierra Leone in West Africa, which still exist today.

It gripped the soul of England

The freedom of spirit that Methodism brought to the working masses of Britain enabled them to 'find their voice' at a time of rapid industrialisation.

Over 150 years later Prime Minister, Lloyd George commented, 'John Wesley inaugurated a movement that gripped the soul of England [and all Britain], that deepened its spiritual instincts, trained them and uplifted them.'(6)

It was just as John Wesley had said: from the root of salvation, good fruit began to grow. Inner transformation of individuals found dynamic expression resulting in an explosion of missionary endeavour away and social reforms at home.

The father of modern missions

During Wesley's lifetime, Captain James Cook had circumnavigated the world, opening the way for a new era of mission. One young Baptist minister, William Carey (1761-1834), inspired by Cook's journals and also by Wesley's missionary vision, was gripped by the command of Jesus to make disciples of all nations. He put his thoughts into print and in 1792 wrote his leaflet, 'An enquiry into the obligations of Christians to use means for the conversion of the heathen.'

When he tried to share what the Holy Spirit was saying to him he was met by resistance: 'Young man, sit down; when God pleases to convert the heathen, he will do it without your aid and mine.' Not to be deterred, he knew he had captured God's heart for the nations and after founding the first missionary society in 1792 he sailed to India. We now know him as the 'father of modern missions' whose watchword was, 'Expect great things from God; attempt great things for God.' (7)

Mission, reform and women

The London Missionary Society (LMS) was started in 1795, the Church

Mission Society (CMS) in 1799, and from thereon too many to mention sprung into existence. The modern mission expansion had begun, and whether the missionaries intended it or not, western cultural values were being promoted at the same time.

Many missionaries were women because they found a voice ministering overseas in ways that British society at home would not allow. Missionary societies welcomed women. During the 19th century, women were also very active in the reform societies which were deemed an acceptable outlet for their 'natural piety,' as long as they weren't too enthusiastic!

God Almighty has set before me...

Five years prior to Carey's revelation of God's heart for the nations, another young man was moved by the Holy Spirit. He wrote in his diary in 1787, 'God Almighty has set before me two great objects, the suppression of the slave trade and the reformation of manners [morals].'(8) This was William Wilberforce (1759-1833).

After his conversion experience, Wilberforce was in two minds whether to become a churchman or remain in politics. It was a conversation with converted slave ship captain, John Newton, that convinced him to use his position in politics to address this institutional evil. So as an MP he embarked on a lifetime campaign to abolish slavery, resulting in the Abolition of the Slave Trade Act in 1807 and the Slavery Abolition Act of 1833.

Even before the acts were passed, Wilberforce was working on behalf of freed slaves in West Africa so they would come to know true freedom in Christ. He was a founding member of the Church Mission Society (CMS) which still exists today. Having found his own faith through reading the Bible, he also played a foundational role in the British and Foreign Bible Society.

Making goodness fashionable

Even following Britain's first awakening, Christianity was in a general decline and those in public life who stood for Christ were ridiculed. Wilberforce was a shining light and helped bring about a reformation of society.

In the early 19th century he was part of a group of other influential men and women called the Clapham Sect (because they lived in Clapham, London) who supported many other reforms as well as each other. They were respectable aristocrats, all members of the Church of England who sought to use their privileged position in society to change it for the good. Their aim, 'to make goodness fashionable' and to bring about 'a reformation of manners,' was just what Wilberforce had written in his diary.

Names, too many to mention

Around this time men and women, far too many to mention, took up humanitarian causes as an expression of their faith. Because people wanted to read the Bible, Robert Raikes began Sunday Schools to teach reading and writing in the 1780s. King George III himself expressed the wish that 'every poor child in my dominion shall be taught to read the Bible.'(9)

Hannah More, a converted playwright, became a high-profile educationalist, and John Howard, one of Wesley's converts, pioneered prison reform. This is to name but a few of the believers who made an impact on society.

A revolution of hearts

While there were the beginnings of social reform in Britain in the late 18th century, it was a different story across the channel. The year 1789 marked the French Revolution and the terror of this must have been fresh in Britain's collective memory for decades, especially for the nobility!

It took a while, but working like leaven, the gospel did its work in people's hearts. As they engaged in the social evils of the day, this revolution of hearts probably stopped Britain from having a bloody revolution. A different Britain was beginning to take shape.

The angel of Christian charity

At Piccadilly Circus, in the heart of London's theatre land, is the landmark monument we know today as 'Eros.' One of the roads that leads from it, Shaftsbury Avenue, gives us a clue who it commemorates. Originally called Anteros, the god of selfless love, it was meant to represent an angel of Christian charity holding an arrow of Christian love piercing the world.

This is a fitting monument to Lord Shaftsbury (1801-1885) who, like Wilberforce before him, used his position and devoted his life to help the underprivileged. It is sad that this monument is now commonly called 'Eros,' the god of erotic love, although it may be quite appropriate to the area it is in.

For the benefit of old England

Shaftsbury deliberately chose to become an MP because he said it 'will give me the best means of doing good. I am bound to try to use what God has put into me for the benefit of old England.'(10) Fifty years of campaigning led to numerous social reforms including the Factory Acts of 1847 and 1853 which reduced (yes, reduced!) the working hours of women and children to 10 hours a day.

This was at the height of Britain's Industrial Revolution and didn't go down well with the exploitative owners of the 'dark satanic mills.'(11) Through legislation he also improved the lot of children in the mines and those working as chimney sweeps. He started 'ragged schools' for the poor and was president of the British and Foreign Bible Society. The Bible was his inspiration and guide throughout his entire life.

In day-to-day life

Shaftsbury's Christianity affected his day-to-day life. One story tells how he allowed a tramp woman to ride inside his carriage while he rode outside with the driver.

On another occasion he gave a 'magic lantern' slide show of the crucifixion at one of his ragged schools to four hundred poor men, women and children. The last slide was of Christ outside a closed door and as weeping was heard in the audience he told them that if they 'opened the door' Christ would 'sup with them.' He wrote, 'There was something so cosy and comfortable in the idea of it, that they came pouring round and thanking me'.(12)

Their lives were prophetic

William Wilberforce and Lord Shaftsbury were two men who spearheaded reforms that changed the face of Britain. What if they had considered politics as too worldly or dirty for a Christian and chosen another course of life? Thankfully, they heard the voice of God and their lives were as prophetic as any revivalist that has ever impacted this nation.

Reform, reform, reform

Following the 1959 revival that took hold of Britain, ensuing decades added fuel to the many bourgeoning social reform movements which were increasingly manned and financed by revivalists. Humanitarianism was seen as essential part of the good news of the gospel.

Dr. Thomas Barnardo saw such poverty in the East End of London that he began orphanages; Josephine Butler successfully campaigned for the repeal of the licensing of vice; people wanted to read the Bible and so there was an increase in the Sunday School movement leading to the Education Act of 1870; the Temperance Movement and Band of Hope sought to address the problem of drunkenness. There seemed to be a society or reform movement for every social ill, and philanthropy was the order of the day.

In darkest England

But our towns and cities still had their dark side. There was an underclass of people who lived in the overcrowded slums. City missions mushroomed and reached out in evangelism and social work.

In 1890, Salvation Army leader, William Booth, wrote a book called, *In Darkest England and the Way Out*.(13) There was talk at the time of 'darkest Africa' but he wanted the British to be aware of the need in their own land. He wrote, 'For darkest Africa as for darkest England there is light beyond,' and appealed to those with wealth to use it for social regeneration.

William and Catherine put their money where their mouth was and devoted their lives to the poor, the prostitutes and criminals. They campaigned for better working conditions, and lobbied against the white slave trade and prostitution.

One quaint idea at the time was to have tea meetings for prostitutes and fallen men. They attracted thousands and Catherine was a noted speaker at these. One advertisement said, 'tea meetings for fallen men – private ticket only, men only of irregular habits, drunkards, tipplers, vicious'!(14)

Londoners loved William and Catherine Booth. At Booth's funeral in 1912 there were 40,000 people who lined the streets. Please pause here and look at the honour this great man was given at his funeral. There are four minutes of actual footage on YouTube.(15)

Building Jerusalem

The Industrial Revolution meant a rise in the middle classes but there was still a huge divide between the haves and the have-nots in late 19th century Britain.

While the Booths were living among the poor, Britain was celebrating her Empire. In 1851 the Great Exhibition at Crystal Palace, London, had showcased the latest technology and brought touches of the exotic from the British Empire. It was visited by a third of the population of Britain and caught the prevailing mood of optimism and social progress.

In line with this Enlightenment thinking, most Christians held a post-millennial, kingdom vision, believing social action would make the world a better place. They were endeavouring to do what William Blake wrote in his famous poem, 'Jerusalem':

I will not cease from mental fight,
Nor shall my sword sleep in my hand:
Till we have built Jerusalem,
In England's green and pleasant land.(16)

From the time of Wesley, the teaching of scriptural holiness as a second blessing had also carried with it the idea of spreading sanctification over the land. It was about eradicating all evils in society, not just the sin and sickness of an individual.

Then there came 'the great reversal'(17) a shift from 'building Jerusalem' to a home 'beyond the blue.'

This world is not my home

This traditional song says it all, 'This world is not my home, I'm just a-passin' through...my treasures are laid up somewhere beyond the blue...the angels beckon me from heaven's open door...and I can't feel at home in this world any more.'

Towards the end of the 19th century, a great shift swept revivalist, evangelical Christianity from a present-kingdom vision to a kingdom that was 'beyond the blue.' Optimistic post-millennialism gave way to pessimistic dispensational premillennialism. It was precipitated by the theology of Brethren founder J.N. Derby and later popularised by the Scofield Reference Bible in 1909.

It became the end-times theology of revivalists and the holiness movement, accepted at the Keswick Conventions and adopted by the 20th century Pentecostal movement. It focused on an imminent rapture, and the task at hand shifted from transforming society to rescuing them from impending peril.

It's summed up in this quote from the great revivalist D.L. Moody in 1899: 'I don't find any place where God says that the world is to grow better and better...I look upon the world as a wrecked vessel, God has given me a lifeboat and said, "Moody, save all you can."'(18)
Half a century before, revivalist Finney had stated that one of the reasons why revivals stop is the failure to be involved in social reform and mission.

A century of missions

While the 19th century was a time of home missions, it was also a time of great missionary expansion abroad and a plethora of mission societies sprung up. One notable couple, Robert and Mary Moffat, spent 62 years in Southern Africa. As the century progressed, missionaries poured into Africa and Asia by their thousands.

In line with Britain's expansionist worldview was the belief that in the providence of God, European nations, especially Britain, had the task of colonising the world to bring about its evangelisation. In the mix was Matthew 24:14, that Christ would come back when the gospel had been preached to all nations. Stir in revival fervour and you have a recipe for a highly motivated missionary.

If any hymn sums up the prevailing attitude to mission, then it's this hymn written in 1886, and incidentally one I sung at Sunday School as a child!

Far, far away in heathen darkness dwelling,
Millions of souls forever may be lost...
Who, who will go, salvation's story telling,
Looking to Jesus, counting not the cost.(19)

Heroes of the hour

Missionaries were the popular heroes of the hour. The intrepid explorations of David Livingstone in Central and East Africa during the 1850s nurtured a romantic, if not idealised, picture of mission.

Tugging at the heartstrings of every would-be missionary were the images invoked by 'the smoke of a thousand villages where no missionary had ever been.'(20) Some were martyred, like John Williams in the South Pacific in 1839, or died alone with fever, but there was no shortage of volunteers to fill the gaps that were left.

From those converted in the mid-century revival, Alexander Mackay was a pioneer missionary to Uganda and Mary Slessor devoted her life to the peoples of Calibar in present-day Nigeria. Both were Scottish, and Livingstone was their hero. Later in the century, Amy Carmichael left Northern Ireland for India where she spent 55 years.

The mantle for Africa

How true it is that our lives can have such a knock-on effect. The young Livingstone was greatly impressed by the Moffats and initially went to work with them in South Africa and even married their daughter, Mary. It was Robert Moffat who encouraged him to venture into the heart of Africa. Then as stories of his adventures filtered through to Britain, many Mackays and Slessors were ready and waiting to take on the mantle for Africa.

Many of these missionaries have had a bad press. Some of their character defects may possibly have excluded them from ministry at home, and their paternalistic attitudes can grate on us in the 21st century. The base of Livingstone's statue at Victoria Falls reads,

'Christianity, Commerce and Civilization' which sums up what some of them were about. Yet they were giants, and let's give them their due honour, not cynicism. After all, we are all children of the era in which we live.

By faith and prayer alone

Faith missions were also rooted in the 1859 revival. During these revival years, a former missionary to China from a Methodist family was working among the poor of the East End of London. His name was Hudson Taylor and because he couldn't bear the thought of one million Chinese a month dying without knowing Jesus, he decided to return to China.

Most missions at the time were directed from Britain, the sending base, but he wanted to direct his work from the field. He learnt his faith principles from George Muller's ministry running huge orphanages in Bristol by faith and prayer alone earlier in the century. The China Inland Mission (CIM) was born in 1865 and Taylor spent 55 years in China.

Unlike most missionaries at that time, those CIM missionaries lived and dressed like the Chinese to identify with them, and to help gain a hearing as they shared the gospel. By 1900 the CIM had 800 missionaries.

Role models to a generation

Another huge faith movement was the Student Volunteer Movement which began in British universities. Young men and women were willing to give up promising careers to go to the ends of the earth. Perhaps the most famous of these were the Cambridge Seven, so called because they were from Cambridge University, who went to the borders of Tibet in 1885 as part of the CIM (now called the Overseas Missionary Fellowship – OMF) and remained missionaries all their lives.

Before leaving, they toured campuses in Britain recruiting and then went on to America, encouraging the movement there. C.T. Studd, a well-known cricketer and one of the seven, gave away his vast inheritance so he could live by faith principles. He was later to be a missionary in India and Africa and founded the World Evangelization Crusade (WEC). They were missionary role models to a generation.

World evangelisation

The rising tide of missionary endeavour continued and reached its zenith in 1910 when the World Missionary Conference was held in Edinburgh, Scotland. It was chaired by John R. Mott, leader of the American Student Volunteer Movement and its motto was, 'The evangelisation of the world in this generation.'(21) It's a comment on the times that there were no non-white indigenous Christians among its 1,200 delegates.

What they didn't know was that in four years' time a world war would slice through Europe and its colonial world. It would effectively snuff out the missions' enterprise and dampen missionary enthusiasm at home. Missionaries who prior to 1914 had worked together on the field, now found themselves in different camps.

A fresh wind blows

It's ironic that no representatives from the Pentecostal revival were invited to Edinburgh. Maybe it was because the missions movement was institutionalising and the new breath of the spirit that was blowing in revival was not welcome. Or perhaps it was because the revival came wrapped in a 'tongues' package that was offensive.

The emerging Pentecostal movement in Britain had been growing since 1907. In the year prior to the Edinburgh Conference, the Pentecostal Missionary Union (PMU) had been started in Sunderland by A.A. Boddy and Cecil Polhill, who was one of the original Cambridge Seven.

Among Christians the idea had been growing that there would be an outpouring of the Holy Spirit for missionary service before the second coming of Christ, which they perceived was imminent. Revivalists and holiness people had linked the second blessing with worldwide revival and placed a great emphasis on foreign mission. The Keswick Convention was noted for its prominent missionary speakers and the challenge they brought.

So when people began to be baptised in the Holy Spirit and spoke in tongues, it was interpreted within this framework.

The power of Pentecost

Jesus told the original 120 that the power of the Holy Spirit would come upon them and they would be witnesses to the ends of the earth (Acts 1:8). So when this outpouring began to happen at various places around the world in the years 1906-7, the mandate was the same.

The latter rain that was falling was to bring in the harvest, and the tongues which accompanied the baptism in the Holy Spirit were initially seen as languages which were given to speed up world evangelisation. As they were 'identified,' that gave a clue to where the missionary was to go.

Some sailed with this understanding, only to be disappointed, and had to get stuck into laborious hours of learning the language of their chosen country. That hope remained, and in fact there are recorded instances of missionaries being understood, but they are few and far between. They tend to be isolated instances, where a message in tongues was given and understood by the indigenous people, or of an unschooled Chinese boy speaking perfect English. (22)

Missionaries of the one-way ticket

This term was used to describe these Pentecostal missionaries that had spoken in tongues and answered the divine call for foreign missions. (23) After being vetted by the PMU, their training was as short as possible. Many sailed to India where there was a similar Pentecostal outpouring, or the Chinese borders of Tibet where Polhill had been.

There was such an urgency to seize this moment in God's calendar. Many went knowing they would never see these shores again, and willing to die in a foreign country unless Jesus returned. Either way, they didn't need return tickets. Some even packed their belongings in a coffin.

Supernatural outfit

These missionaries carried the Pentecostal revival with them. Their main job was to save souls and get them filled with the Holy Spirit and to speak in tongues. They were at all times to carry what Boddy called their 'supernatural outfit,'(24) the gifts of the Spirit. Divine healing was at the foundation of their work, and through confrontation or power encounters with traditional healers many converts were won. It is rather like the encounters which helped evangelise our nation.

They questioned, what was the point in making this world a better place if Jesus was coming back any minute? But that didn't mean that Pentecostal mission, whether home or away, didn't have a social aspect. Because of the love for humanity that God had placed in their hearts, there were educational projects, care for orphans and work in slums.

Just for the record, Pentecostal theology has evolved from those early beginnings and Pentecostal missionaries are having an amazing impact in today's world. They've moved from 'bringing in the sheaves' to 'bringing in the kingdom'!

From church to state
Just over a thousand years ago the Christian king of the Anglo-Saxons, Alfred the Great, wrote, 'There is only one way by which to build any kingdom and that is on the sure and certain foundation of faith in Jesus Christ, and in Jesus Christ crucified, and it is on that foundation that I intend to build my kingdom.'(25)

Through the vicissitudes of centuries, Christian ideals and values have been the salt that has preserved British society.

In more recent history, Trade Unionism had its roots in revivalist Christianity. The man that inspired the movement that led to the formation of the Labour party, Keir Hardie, was a Christian, as was the first Labour Prime Minister, Ramsey MacDonald. Christian ideals moved from church to state.

I'm not making any political point but to say that these, like others, stand in the line of Wilberforce and Shaftsbury. They were men and women who have chosen politics as an expression of their faith. Some still do so, up to the present day, and deserve the same honour.

Releasers of goodness
We are a blessed nation. Let that sink in for a moment: we are blessed! With all the social and political issues we face, God has been good to us. It could have been so different.

As Christians we are blessed so that we can be a blessing. That is the gospel (Genesis 12:1, Galatians 3:5). Almost 300 years ago Wilberforce wanted to 'make goodness fashionable.' I like that. He and men and women like him released goodness over this land and brought about the beginnings of a transformation. Imagine if every Christian today became an intentional releaser of goodness!

A land of his hope and his glory

When Moses asked to see God's glory, God showed him his goodness (Exodus 33:19). When we release goodness we are releasing God's glory.

We have it in our power to redeem the words of what has become an alternative national anthem, 'Land of Hope and Glory,'(26) first published in 1902. We don't look to the hope of enlightenment or the glory of empire, but interpret it prophetically. It is the hope there is to be found in Jesus Christ, and the glory of God that will cover the earth.

Missions, both home and away, meet at this point.

For the earth will be filled with the knowledge of the glory of the Lord,
as the waters cover the sea.
Habakkuk 2:14

Endnotes

1. Allen Anderson, *Signs and Blunders*, article, www.artsweb.bham.ac.uk/aanderson/Publications/signs_and_blunders.htm

2. http://www.goodreads.com/author/quotes/151350.John_Wesley

3. A. Skevington Wood, *The Burning Heart*, Cliff College, Sheffield, UK, 2001, p 142.

4. Ibid., pp 141-2.

5. Ibid., p 106.

6. David E. Gardner, *The Trumpet Sounds for Britain*, Jesus is Alive Ministries, Southend on Sea, UK, 2010, p 90.

7. For an overview of Carey's life and ministry including quotes referred to, www.wholesomewords.org/mission.bcarey3.htm

8.http://www.chinstitute.org/wp-content/themes/cms/pdfmodules/wilberforce.pdf

9. http://internationalwallofprayer.org/Q-01-FAMOUS-QUOTES.html

10. *Heroes of the Faith*, Issue 6, April-June 2011, New Life Publishing, Nottingham, UK, p 28.

11. From *Jerusalem*, William Blake, 1804.

12. Heroes of the Faith, op.cit., p 29.

13. William Booth, *In Darkest England and the Way Out*, Salvation Army Publishing, 1890, www.jesus.org.uk/vault/library/booth_darkest_england.pdf

14. J Edwin Orr, *The Second Evangelical Awakening in Britain*, Marshall, Morgan and Scott, London, Edinburgh, UK, 1949, p 169.

15. www.youtube.com/watch?v=-Mp9OkRcMY8

16. William Blake, op.cit

17. David J. Bosch, *Transforming Mission*, Orbis, New York, USA, 1998, p 318.

18. Ibid., p 318

19. James McGranahan, 1886.

20. www.wholesomewords.org/mission/giants/biolivingstone/html

21. Mott wrote a book of this name in 1905.

22. Confidence, 1908-26, letters 'from our missionaries' contain various stories.

23. Vinson Synan, *The Spirit Said 'Grow,'* MARC, Monrovia, USA, 1992, p 39-48.

24. Confidence, March 1910, pp 69-72.

25. Gardner, op.cit., p 44.

26. H.C. Benson, *Land of Hope and Glory*, 1902.

9
Inheriting the Blessings

He remembers his covenant forever, the word he commanded, for a
thousand generations
1 Chronicles 16:15, Psalm 105:8

History is *his*-story

What you have read is really his-story. It shows how God has worked
in human history in one small island of the world. Just think how many
times similar stories can be multiplied across the nations!

When William Carey was told that God could convert the heathen
without his help, he understood that God works in relationship with his
people. God wants his children to know him, to listen to his voice and
creatively work in partnership with him to bring about the restoration
of this planet.

Our world is still groaning, waiting for its liberation (Romans 8:22-
23). Adam and Eve's job description is still ours – to *'be fruitful and*
increase in number; fill the earth and subdue it. Rule over the fish in the
sea and the birds in the sky and over every living creature that moves
on the ground' (Genesis 1:28).

What an amazing heritage we have.

Grace and favour

I hope that by now you will have been captivated by the favour that

God has poured out on these little islands. Our land has a story to tell and a history with God. I have endeavoured to cut a shaft down through time to our foundations. I've tunnelled through the rock and allowed our eyes to take a glimpse at *'all its treasures'* (Job 28:10), exposing the *'ancient ruins'* and *'age-old foundations'* that need rebuilding (Isaiah 58:12).

Nowhere has been left out of God's gracious outpourings of his Spirit. The land has heard the words of the Lord from Land's End to John O'Groats and from East Anglia to Ulster. It would be almost impossible to substantiate, but I wouldn't be surprised if every city, town and village had been visited by God's holy presence at some time in its history.

Job 12:2 says, *'Speak to the earth and it will teach you.'* I sometimes wonder whether land that has known the heavy presence of God descending has something to say, as if the very stones are waiting to cry out and give up their secrets (Luke 19:40).

I said in the introduction that history can impact the present when it is given a biblical and prophetic perspective, so that's what I'm going to turn to.

A journey of discovery

I love going on a journey of discovery with the Lord. When we involve the Holy Spirit in what we are doing and thinking, it's exciting, and we never know where the signposts are going to point to next.

Our personal stories are given significance as we partner with him and allow our lives to become part of his big story. He is always finding ways to encourage us, and one way of doing this is through the prophetic.

I'd been researching the Pentecostal revival in Britain for my first book,(1) and on the first Sunday of 2004 I had a prophetic word that shifted me up to another gear in revelation.

I was spending Christmas and New Year in Pasadena, California and that morning I attended a church I had never been to before. During the ministry time at the end, I was at the front of the auditorium with hundreds of others and I received a prophecy from one of the leaders whom I happened to recognise.

As he released the prophecy over me it was as if liquid fire like a flowing destiny was being poured over my head. I'd never felt anything like it before, nor have I since.

Covenant is the key

These are some of the main things that the prophecy contained:

Covenant is the key to opening up the wells in the UK. Zipporah (Exodus 4:24-5) was a woman of covenant, and she upheld the covenant. God wants to raise up Zipporahs. God wants to raise up a bride to uphold the covenant, just as he raised up Zipporah. Just as this was a key to bringing about a great deliverance for Moses, so this is a key to bringing about a great deliverance for Britain.

Zipporah was a warrior of the covenant. This key, the raising up of Zipporahs, will bring about a renewal of the covenant. This move will touch kings and queens.

Then the leader prophesied spoke about the wells of Azusa and of Parham, Seymour and of Bartleman transferred to Sunderland and that same mantle resting on A.A. Boddy.(2) He went on to say that the covenant God made at Azusa, he made at Sunderland:

The wells are there. God wants to renew that covenant, to pour out his Spirit over the UK just as he did at the turn of the century (1900).

He then spoke about the significance of Shechem, Israel, in covenant renewal. He prophesied that I would be instrumental in this.

I felt this being spoken straight into my Spirit. The Monday before Christmas I had spent a day with the Lord sitting by a swimming pool with the mountains of Altadena above me and during one of those special times, he began to speak to me. I wrote down the revelations that seemed to pour from the Scriptures. What I wrote was all about covenant, Zipporah and Shechem.

Afterwards this prophetic word I spoke to the person who had given it to me and told him what the Lord had said to me. He said that I must pursue this as I was definitely on to something.

It's very easy to put your own interpretation on prophetic words and I've tried to be careful not to do this. It has sent me to the Lord and his word, and for the last eight years I feel I have been getting more pieces of the puzzle. As I've put them together, it has made a picture of what it looks like to unblock and re-dig the wells, and understand our spiritual inheritance.

What follows in this chapter and the next are some of the ideas that were birthed that day sitting at the poolside, and confirmed in that prophetic word.

I will be their God

Covenant is not one of those words we use every day, but it was and still is the way God relates to his people. It's born out of his deep desire for relationship. The Old Testament contains a series of covenants that God made with the Israelites, the people he called his *'treasured possession'* (Deuteronomy 14:2).

In the covenant formula that keeps on cropping up, he says, *'I will be your God and you will be my people'* (Jeremiah 31:33). This followed the custom at that time where two people, tribes or nations would make a binding agreement with each other, laying out terms that each party had to adhere to.

The covenant would frequently be sealed with blood and was binding to both parties if the conditions were met. There were blessings for keeping the terms of the covenant, and curses for disobedience. You can read something about this in Deuteronomy 27 and 28.

As you read through the Old Testament you can't help being struck by God's amazing faithfulness and love towards his people, the Israelites, even though so often they turned their back on him and *'worshipped the gods of the people around them'* (Judges 2:12). Sound familiar?

To a thousand generations

Those who read the Bible through 'grace-healed eyes' (3) and not through a lens of judgement can see the thread of blessing from Genesis to Revelation. This grace always triumphs over judgement (James 2:13).

Blessings are more powerful than curses and are meant to extend to a thousand generations, a way of saying that they never end. *'Know therefore that the Lord your God is God; he is the faithful God, keeping his covenant of love to a thousand generations of those who love him and keep his commands'* (Deuteronomy 7:9). In the first chapter of Genesis, God released blessing on the first man and woman: *'God blessed them and said to them, be fruitful and increase in number; fill the earth and subdue it'* (Genesis 1:28).

Our heavenly Dad wanted to lavish his love on his children. Even through the dark days that followed the fall (Genesis 2-11), God's purpose remained the same and has never changed. He wanted a people through whom all nations of the world could be blessed and made a covenant with Abraham to this end: *'I will bless you...and you will be a blessing...all peoples on earth will be blessed through you'* (Genesis 12:2-3).

It's the gospel!

God yearned for relationship with mankind. I believe satisfaction settled in his heart as this covenant was sealed and he put his inheritance laws into operation, that Abraham's descendants would inherit the land of Canaan as a down-payment on the 'all peoples mandate' (Genesis 13:14-17, 15:18).

God who said, *'I will be their God, they will be my people'* (Jeremiah 31:33) is still saying that today. This is the Gospel. It's the good news of blessing and we are even told that the gospel was *'announced...in advance to Abraham'* (Galatians 3:8).

As the priests under the old covenant mediated between God and his people, they were to release their priestly blessing on them. *'The Lord bless you and keep you; the Lord make his face shine upon you and be gracious to you; the Lord turn his face towards you and give you peace'* (Numbers 6:24-26).

God wanted them to understand that as they fully obeyed the laws he gave them they would be 'overtaken by blessing.' Just read the list in Deuteronomy 28:1-14! Who wouldn't want that? But covenant breaking had a consequence and the covenant curse would come into operation if they were disobedient (Deuteronomy 28:15-68).

A love story

At various important milestones of the nation, Israel gathered together. In a covenant renewal ceremony, the history of God's faithfulness was remembered and they pledged allegiance to be his people.

It was always linked with taking the land, such as when they were about to enter the Promised Land (Deuteronomy 28-29), when they had their first conquest in Canaan (Joshua 8:3-35), and when the conquest of the land was complete (Joshua 24:1-27). After the exile in Babylon and they returned to their land again, there was another covenant renewal in the days of Nehemiah and Ezra (Nehemiah 9).

The Old Testament story is really a love story of how God wooed back an unfaithful people. He drew them with cords of love, keeping his side of the covenant. It was the assignment of the Old Testament prophets to keep the king, and thus the country, in line with the covenantal responsibilities so the nation would live in blessing.

Inheritors of blessing

God spoke through the prophets that one day it would be different, that there would be another covenant he would make with his people (Ezekiel 33:24-28, Jeremiah 31:31-34). Today we no longer live under the Old Covenant but we still live in covenantal relationship with God, in the New Covenant.

Under the terms of the New Covenant, it's not what we do or don't do, how obedient or disobedient we are, it's not about keeping a set of rules and regulations, that's just religion. It's about what Jesus has done.

He was perfectly obedient. He kept the covenant and because of that we can just enter into all the blessings. What's more, on the cross, Jesus sealed the New Covenant with his own blood and made a way for the Holy Spirit to live in us forever. It's a win-win situation!

When we catch hold of this, we will know what it is to live in freedom, not under a cloud of condemnation but just enjoying life with a capital L, lived in relationship with a good God who smiles down upon us and says, 'I am your God, you are my people!' This is a truth that needs to sink right down in our spirits because it will change the way we live. It needs to be taken hold of by faith, the currency of the kingdom. Today we are the inheritors of blessing. When we have this revelation the blessings belong to us (Deuteronomy 29:29). We are made for blessing!

From the fullness of his grace

I came across some thoughts recently that have really helped me appreciate this more fully.(4) Overcome by the sheer revelation of just who Jesus was and what his coming to mankind means, John says, *'From the fullness of his grace we have all received one blessing after another. For the law was given through Moses; grace and truth came through Jesus Christ'* (John 1:16-17).

I always read that as a double-edged sword, grace verses the truth but the phrase 'grace and truth' literally means 'God's unconditional love and faithfulness to the covenant.' The 'fullness' refers to the presence of God in Jesus Christ. It's not the law, the Torah pitted against grace.

Moses gave the Torah but Jesus was the Torah. God's fullness entered the world (Colossians 1:19) and he is not only looking for containers to fill but to ultimately fill the world with his glory (Habakkuk 2:14).

So what's this all got to do with Britain's spiritual heritage? The answer is everything!

From glory to glory

The blessings that have been unleashed on Britain from his fullness, the revelations and the revivals, were never meant to end. We are always meant to go from glory to glory. Each succeeding generation is supposed to build on what was revealed or accomplished in the previous generation.

Even if past moves of God seem dry, dead and even buried, where the life that birthed a revival is now relegated to religious formulas, and truths that were once new and exciting revelations have become doctrinal dogma, we as New Covenant believers can by faith claim those past blessings as our inheritance. All of them...pause here and ponder that for a while! Remember, God keeps his covenant of love to a thousand generations. So how do we make that connection?

The ebb and flow of revival

No other book in the Bible illustrates the ebb and flow of revivals like the book of Judges. There were times when the Israelites forgot their amazing history and followed the gods of the people around them. When things got too bad they cried out to God for help, and faithful to his covenant he answered.

God sent men (and in one case a woman), called judges, five in all, to rescue them and bring them back to God. It is rather like a revival draws people back to the Lord, following an individual or group's powerful encounter with God. The cycles repeated themselves and when the judge died, the people went back to their own ways.

One of these judges was Gideon. His story in Judges 6–8 tells how he delivered Israel from the Midianites who lived across Israel's border and continually invaded their land. During his lifetime there was peace and Gideon was re-named Jerub-Baal (let Baal contend with him) because he had destroyed his father's altar to Baal and raised an army to defeat the enemy. He was certainly a force to be reckoned with.

They didn't remember

It's a familiar story, but less familiar is what happened after Gideon died. I want to use this part of the story to give us some keys to help us be good stewards of our spiritual history, so we can keep present revivals rolling.

Gideon had seventy sons and one illegitimate son called Abimelech. Abimelech set himself up as king and killed all his brothers, except for Jotham who escaped. The cycle of apostasy was beginning to repeat itself.

No sooner had Gideon died than the Israelites prostituted themselves to the Baals. They set up Baal-Berith as their god and did not remember the Lord their God, who had rescued them from the hands of all their enemies on every side. They also failed to show kindness to the family of Jerub-Baal (that is, Gideon) for all the good things he had done for them. (Judges 8:33-35)

Baal-Berith means 'god of the covenant,' so in effect the Israelites were rejecting their covenantal privileges and responsibilities with the God of Israel and pledging their allegiance to a false god in exchange for his favour and protection. Baal's temple was at Shechem, a really significant place in Israelite history connected with covenant and its associated blessings and curses.

The covenant curse

Moving on with the story, Jotham, the escaped brother, shouted to the citizens of Shechem in the form of a parable saying that they had given up oil, fruit and wine for thorns. It was a sad state of affairs (Judges 9:7-20). Jotham cursed Shechem and its inhabitants from Mount Gerizim.

This was the same mountain where the tribes were to pronounce blessings over the people at the covenant renewals. What an irony! He said that they had acted dishonourably and that fire would consume the people and the city.

Abimelech governed three more years before the curse came into effect. The citizens of Shechem turned against him and Abimelech was ousted from his position. He retaliated by attacking Shechem and killing all its inhabitants. Destroying the city, he threw salt over it condemning it to perpetual barrenness and desolation, in keeping with the covenant curse.

Those citizens that escaped fled to the temple of Baal-Berith which Abimelech burned with fire, killing about a thousand women and children. The god of the false covenant had offered no protection at all.

Flowing down the generations

This story illustrates how the covenantal blessings were cut off. First of all, the people chose to reject the God of Israel and the covenant and follow Baal (Judges 8:33). Secondly, they didn't remember their history, thirdly, they didn't value their inheritance, and finally, they didn't honour their fathers (Judges 8:35)

So the converse is true if we want the blessings to flow down the generations...it's simple. Firstly, live in the light of the New Covenant (we've looked at that), secondly, remember our history with God, thirdly, value our inheritance, and lastly honour our fathers (and mothers) in the faith. These are key things to remember when looking at our own history and give us an approach to the past to help us unblock and re-digging the wells of blessing.

The significance of Shechem

Looking at this story, I was fascinated by the place, Shechem, which acted as a backdrop for this drama. It acts as a metaphor for places of past revival, places where the Lord appeared and altars were built; places of covenant.

It all began when the Lord appeared to Abraham at Shechem and promised him and his descendants the land of Canaan. Abraham responded by building an altar (Genesis 12:7). In a prophetic act, Jacob, his grandson, brought some land there as a down-payment of his promised inheritance. He pitched his tent and dug a well (Genesis 33:18). There in the middle of pagan territory he made the declaration, 'God, the God of Israel is mighty.'

Jacob gave this land to his son, Joseph, who insisted that one day his bones were taken back from Egypt to be buried there (Genesis 50:25, Exodus 13:19). In turn, this tract of land at Shechem became the inheritance for Joseph's descendants as the centre of the tribes Ephraim and Manasseh (Joshua 24:32).

A place of inheritance

Well aware of this, just as the Israelites stood on the threshold of the Promised Land, before they crossed the Jordan, Moses renewed the covenant at Shechem. Standing between Mount Ebal and Mount Gerizim (Deuteronomy 27-29), he read all the associated blessings and curses.

After the battles of Ai and Jericho, early on in their conquest of the land, Joshua gathered the tribes and renewed the covenant at Shechem (Joshua 8:30). Again when the job was done he gathered the tribes at Shechem and the covenant was renewed again.

Shechem was a place of inheritance, a geographic location which symbolised the covenantal blessings cascading down the generations. This stood in stark contrast to Abimelech's attempt of a Canaanite revival at the same place.

The water still flows

I believe that Jesus knew what he was doing when he went to drink from Jacob's well at Sychar, in the vicinity of Shechem (John 4:4-26). Although the city had been destroyed and the land cursed with salt, the well remained, and the water below the ground still flowed.

Fourth-century pilgrims mention this well as being 100 feet deep. When it was cleaned out in 1935 it was 138 feet deep, and today it is 75 feet deep. Sometimes it had been forgotten but it's still there!

It's as if the well provided generational continuity and showed that underneath it all, the covenant continues, waiting to be renewed. Under our nation the spiritual water is still there and wells exist. The covenant that our forefathers made with God is up for renewal.

This well had refreshed generations and the Samaritan lady was drinking in that line of succession. The covenant of blessing that God made with Abraham was now springing up afresh. In this encounter Jesus was opening up a whole new understanding of spiritual inheritance from a New Covenant perspective.

No more curse, only blessing. What a significant place to release living water to bless the world!

The New Covenant no longer comes with strings attached, as the old did. We don't have to go back time and again to draw water, but the living water that Jesus gives is a continuous flow from deep within us.

So where's a starting place to explore our inheritance? Look for the 'Shechems!'

Each believer's covenant

Already in this book we have seen so many places and movements that could be considered 'Shechems,' rather like the memorial stones in Canaan we read about in Chapter 1. The initiators, the spiritual movers and shakers of their generations, had captured a portion of heaven and brought it to earth.

These leaders were wired with divine purpose. They knew that God was their God and that they were his people and they lived in covenant partnership. As we unearth their original vision and catch their heart, it's all part of entering into the covenant God made with our forefathers, a covenant renewal. John Wesley understood the importance of covenant renewal and used this prayer in services for the renewal of the believer's covenant with God. It is still used by Methodists today.(5)

> I am no longer my own, but yours.
> Put me to what you will, rank me with whom you will;
> put me to doing, put me to suffering.
> Let me be employed by you or laid aside by you,
> enabled for you or brought low by you.
> Let me be full, let me be empty.
> Let me have all things, let me have nothing.
> I freely and heartily yield all things
> to your pleasure and disposal.
> And now, O glorious and blessed God,
> Father, Son, and Holy Spirit,
> you are mine, and I am yours. So be it.
> And the covenant which I have made on earth,
> let it be ratified in heaven.
> Amen.

Earthing the fire

There is something I don't fully understand in regard to location. I believe that God can be worshipped anywhere in spirit and in truth, yet there can be no denying that sometimes he chooses to manifest himself more strongly in particular places and people, at particular times.

If we take the analogy of lightning, this can flash across the sky accompanied by the rumble of thunder and heavy rain. The rain falls and soaks anyone who walks outside. The thunder is heard by anyone in earshot of the storm, yet the lightening is attracted to specific places where the electricity it contains can be earthed. This can result in its power flowing through anything or anyone unfortunate enough to be hit, possibly resulting in fire.

In the same way, the powerful effect of the Spirit finds an earth at specific places and people. I am reminded of the scripture in 2

Chronicles 16:9 which says, *'The eyes of the Lord roam throughout the earth to strengthen those whose hearts are fully committed to him.'* There also seem to be certain places where the soil has been prepared through past moves of God, or certain conditions have come together, ready to receive the fire.

Throughout our history God has often moved in the same place more than once.

Following the Welsh Revival in 1905, over 3,000 were converted in Kingswood, the area of Bristol where five generations earlier, Wesley and Whitefield had had their greatest successes.(6)

In 1921 as Christians in Lowestoft prayed for revival, the record says that 'Those with a sense of history would remember how God worked before.' That was during the second evangelical awakening in 1861. And he did again. (7)

Sundered by the river

One place in Britain that has had consistent visitations of God is Sunderland, on the north east coast of England. The name of this town has been cropping up throughout this book. The city is cut in two as the River Wear flows through it into the North Sea. It is indeed a 'land sundered by the river' – what a prophetic statement!

The river of God has flowed through that place since the very beginnings of Christianity in England. One side of the river is called Monkwearmouth (monks at the mouth of the Wear) and the other side Bishopwearmouth (land originally owned by the bishops of Durham).

Bede, who wrote the exhaustive history of the coming of Christianity to Britain, spent his life in the vicinity of Monkwearmouth at the twin monasteries of St. Peter and St. Paul, which was at nearby Jarrow. This was in the seventh century and it was thirteen centuries later that the Pentecostal Revival began at All Saints Church in the Parish of Monkwearmouth just a stone's throw away from Bede's monastery.

Vicar A.A. Boddy knew his heritage when he said, 'The Lord has had his witnesses in Monkwearmouth through the ages.'(8) Whether it was the Quakers, Methodists, the 'Prims,' the Salvation Army or visits by revivalists, James Caughey, Phoebe Palmer, George Jeffries and others, Sunderland had been fertile soil with huge numbers responding to the gospel. More recently the wells were opened as it was a main centre in Britain for the 'Toronto Blessing.'

The prophecy I received in Pasadena said that the Azusa wells dug by William Seymour in 1906 under the influence and teachings of Charles Parham and by Frank Bartleman were transferred to Sunderland, and the same mantle of leadership of the Pentecostal revival in the States rested on A.A. Boddy. I believe the wells are still there and although they are very deep, the water is very near the surface.

Digging makes the difference

What was laid in the foundations of your town, city or village? I found out the other day that Eccles was an ecclesiastical centre founded by the Romans. What was the vision of the founding fathers? Is there a work of God that's been left unfinished or a move of God that fizzled out? Was there anything of significance that happened in the place?

Ask God the question, 'What did you want to accomplish here?' Is there a mantle to be picked up? A little digging makes the difference and you may discover God's redemptive purpose that you can pick up again and run with.

There are many more Shechems where the fountains of the deep will once again meet the floodgates of heaven. Then the water of life will be released top down and bottom up!

Long ago

If we return to Gideon, we will see that after his death the people didn't remember their history and that was one reason the blessings were cut off (Judges 8:35).

In the ancient near east, it was important to recount the past history of relationship between the two parties before making or reaffirming covenant commitments. In the case of the Israelites, it involved recalling God's faithfulness over many generations. It was an encouragement that what God has done before, he can do again.

After the conquest of Canaan, Joshua gathered the tribes at Shechem (Joshua 24). They presented themselves before God, and Joshua, under prophetic inspiration, began with the words, 'Long ago.'

There followed a discourse, spoken from God's perspective, which would have powerfully reminded them of their relational history with their God beginning with Abraham up to the present. The people pledged their allegiance to serve the Lord and keep the covenant. Only then did Joshua send them back to consolidate the victories won in the land.

Years later when the exiles returned from Babylon, Nehemiah gathered the people together (Nehemiah 9) and reminded them of God's amazing faithfulness and love despite their disobedience. It inspired faith for the new day and gave them a new chance for them to 'be his people and for God to be their God.'

Nehemiah captured something key to the heart of God when he described Him as, *'a forgiving God, gracious and compassionate, slow to anger and abounding in love'* (Nehemiah 9:17). Even in the face of Israel's unfaithfulness, instead of punishment for the sins of the fathers to the third and forth generations, God is revealed as a God who keeps a covenant of love to a thousand generations who love him and keep is commands. (Deuteronomy 7:9) It was if God was already coming from a New Covenant perspective, reaching forward in time and claiming what was reserved for another day. Blessings outweigh curses!

To all afar off

On the day of Pentecost, Peter spontaneously asserted, *'Men of Israel, listen to this...'* He went on to give a short account of their own history, to show that Jesus is indeed the Messiah fulfilling the covenant made to their 'father' King David (Acts 2:22-36). They were now heirs to the blessings of the New Covenant as they embraced their Messiah and received the gift of the Holy Spirit. Peter affirms that the outpouring of the Spirit was not just for that generation but *'for [their] children and for all who are far off'* (Acts 2:39).

We stand in that line and as we tell the stories of past moves of God, it's as if we are celebrating a corporate covenant renewal. We are remembering, and in our remembering become recipients of blessing and the gift of the Holy Spirit.

Gathering of the saints

Wherever the early Pentecostals in Britain met following the revival in 1907, they saw themselves in a line of Spirit-filled believers, a remnant that had existed throughout the ages since Peter's declaration. A scripture that was often quoted in their gatherings was Psalm 50:5 (KJV), *'Gather my saints together unto me; those that have made a covenant with me by sacrifice.'* They understood covenant as a key to release the river of his Spirit from the past to the present.

Wakey, wakey!

There are blessings available for us, if we are prepared to rouse ourselves! Louise is a young woman from Llanelly, South Wales, a few miles away from Moriah Chapel, home of the Welsh Revival. Having attended Bethel School of Supernatural Ministry, Redding, California for three years, she tells this story:

I got woken up in the night because there was such a strong presence of God in my bedroom. I told God I was listening and he said to me, 'I want you to go to Moriah Chapel and say, 'Wakey, wakey.' I knew that if I didn't do it I would regret it for the rest of my life and would wonder what would have happened.

One day after I finished college, I walked over to the chapel. When I got there, there were a few people standing outside. After a little while of building up courage, I said, 'Wakey, wakey' very quietly because I was so embarrassed. Straightaway God said to me, 'Is that how much you want revival in Wales?' I told him, 'No,' and that I wanted it way more than that, so he told me to say it louder. After a couple of minutes I shouted, 'Wakey, wakey' at the chapel at the top of my voice.

Nothing happened for a few minutes so I turned around and was going to cross the road. When I had my back to the chapel the ground started to shake and I heard a huge yawn. I was freaked out because I had no idea what was happening and a part of me didn't want to turn around but just run off down the road. But I did, I turned around and faced the chapel.

When I did, a huge angel stepped out of the chapel. He was HUGE! All I could see was his feet. I tried to see his face but I couldn't put my head back far enough. I can't remember if I asked him who he was or whether he just started speaking to me. I'm pretty sure I asked him, 'Who are you?' All I can really remember is being shocked and kind of dazed because I couldn't believe what had just happened.

He started speaking and said to me, 'I'm the angel from the 1904 revival and you have just woken me up.' I then remember being kind of confused because I thought angels didn't sleep! He went on to say that he had fallen asleep because people had stopped calling out for revival. He then started walking down the road and I went and sat on a bench for what must have been four hours trying to figure out and process what had just happened.

A story like that might be outside your grid, but I like the idea of angels all around Britain ready to be woken up to complete their assignments! Weird? But so is the story of Ezekiel speaking to old, dry bones to bring them to life (Ezekiel 37:1-10).

Scrolls of remembrance

In our remembering we are unrolling God's scroll of remembrance (Malachi 3:16) and as we talk with each other about what God has done for his people, he listens and hears. Reminiscing can be pure nostalgia. I'm not talking about just harking back to 'the good old days.'

Remembering is like ploughing back spiritual nutrients into the soil of our individual and corporate spiritual lives. Every act of remembrance breathes life into the flame burning on the altar that should never go out (Leviticus 6:13).

Remember our history...value our inheritance...honour our fathers.

Then those who feared the Lord talked with each other, and the Lord listened and heard. A scroll of remembrance was written in his presence concerning those who feared the Lord and honoured his name.

(Malachi 3:16)

Endnotes

1. Diana Chapman, *Searching the Source of the River, The Forgotten Women of the Pentecostal Revival in Britain*, Push Publishing, London, UK, 2007.

2. Revd. A.A. Boddy was the vicar of All Saints' Church, Monkwearmouth, Sunderland which was the hub of the Pentecostal Revival in Britain, 1907-1914.

3. Philip Yancey, *What's So Amazing About Grace*, Zondervan, Grand Rapids, USA, 1997, p 161.

4. Jean-Jacques Suurmond, *Word and Spirit at Play*, SCM Press, London, UK, 1994, p 108.

5. http://www.methodist.org.uk

6. J. Edwin Orr, *The Flaming Tongue*, Moody Press, Chicago, USA, 1973, p 40.

7. Stanley Griffin, *A Forgotten Revival*, Day One Publications, Bromley, UK, 1992, pp 101,121.

8. *Confidence*, May 1911, p 120.

10
Connecting the Generations

Preaching was in his blood

John Wesley once said, 'If I were to write my own life, I should begin before I was born.'(1) He stood in a line of preachers dating back to his great-grandfather who was a Puritan, and for that reason was removed as rector of his parish in 1662. After that, he preached in nonconformist chapels in the area of Dorset where he lived.

It sounds like a familiar story since his great-grandson John travelled the same path and found himself unwelcome in the established churches. You could say that preaching and nonconformity was in John Wesley's blood.

No one is excluded

I've told the story of the prophecy that encouraged me on my journey of discovery, but it was also prophecy that got me started. It was 1996, the second year of the 'Toronto Blessing' outpouring and we had a visiting prophet from Toronto at our church. Unlike the prophecy I received in Pasadena, this one neither confirmed nor resonated with anything going on with me at that time.

He told me that there was revival in my blood and I needed to do some digging because there were great men and women of God in my past who shook towns. He went on to say, 'Di, you've been called into this.' This puzzled me because as far as I knew I was the only Christian in my family, apart from an old aunt and my late uncle who had been a lay preacher. In fact, when he had wanted to study theology he had been actively opposed by the rest of the family. I called my Aunt Jean and she was as puzzled as me. It was one of those prophesies that wouldn't go away but I really didn't understand it.

It wasn't until seven years later that the lights came on! It was simple. Once we are 'born of the Spirit' (John 3:5) we enter the large extended family of God with ancestors too many to number. My bloodline can be traced back to Christ, and my spiritual DNA has in it portions of heaven which men and women of God in the past have laid hold of.

This is my spiritual inheritance and as the prophecy said, 'I've been called into this.' So have you!

It's great if you have a natural godly inheritance like Wesley, and if that's the case, I encourage you to claim every one of the blessings that are yours. But the Father I know is inclusive and has adopted me. He says that it is the glory of kings to search out a matter. I believe he's loved watching me 'do the digging' to discover who I am, and understand that I can claim by faith all the blessings that belong to me.

Zipporah, woman of covenant

The prophecy I received in Pasadena talked a lot about Zipporah as a woman and warrior of the covenant. It went on to say that God wants to raise up a bride to uphold the covenant just as he raised up Zipporah. Just as this was a key to bringing about a great deliverance for Moses, so this is a key to bringing about a great deliverance for Britain.

So what's the story here? After the burning bush encounter with the Lord, Moses was on his way back to Egypt to deliver his people from slavery. He had been in Midian working as a shepherd and while there had married Zipporah, the daughter of a Midianite priest.

There is a surprising incident after this mandate from the Lord. At a lodging place on the way back to Egypt, the Lord met Moses and was about to kill him because he had not performed his duty as a father and circumcised his son. We read that Zipporah *'took a flint knife, cut off her son's foreskin and touched Moses' feet with it...and the Lord let him alone'* (Exodus 4:25). Moses then went on to be the deliverer of his people. This is a short and seemingly rather bizarre story, but it is one of significance.

Valuing our inheritance

The sign of the covenant was circumcision. God had instructed Abraham, *'My covenant in your flesh is to be an everlasting covenant. Any uncircumcised male who has not been circumcised in the flesh, will be cut off from his people; he has broken my covenant'* (Genesis 17:13-14).

After Gideon died, the people who had been beneficiaries of the deliverance he brought about disregarded their godly inheritance. Not so Zipporah. Even though as Moses wife she married into the covenant rather than being born into it, she valued her family's godly inheritance and understood the significance of the covenant.

Interestingly, she was a Midianite, the tribe that Gideon defeated. At all costs she was going to make sure that the covenantal blessings of Israel would cascade down the generations to her sons. It was the cutting of the organ of fertility that guaranteed generational succession.

Zipporah, then, acts as a metaphor for us as the bride of Christ. We need to understand and value covenant as well as know its significance in our spiritual inheritance. It is one thing to know the stories of our heritage, but it is another to value them.

When King Ahab wanted to buy Naboth's vineyard, Naboth's answer was, *'The Lord forbid that I should give you the inheritance of my fathers'* (1 Kings 21:3). He valued his inheritance and would not let it be robbed from him, even though it cost him his life.

A father's blessing

Contrast this with Esau who was willing to sell his birthright just because he was hungry and wanted a bowl of stew in a hurry. And think of the extent of trickery and deception that Jacob resorted to, to acquire it and receive old Isaac's blessing (Genesis 27). Once given, it could not be taken from him, and Esau had to live with that remorse.

Jacob valued his inheritance. The last chapters of Genesis paint a picture of a mellowed Jacob, now called Israel, a prince with God. Old and leaning upon his staff, he passed on the father's blessing to his twelve children. Under the Old Covenant, a father's blessing was something to be highly valued. It was a vehicle for generational continuity.

Esau didn't think generationally; he just wanted to satisfy his immediate hunger. He lost out because he lived only in the now. We can lose out if we don't appreciate that we stand in a spiritual generational line that goes back millennia.

Royalty in the kingdom

British royalty is built on generational succession, with a deep understanding of family history and favoured status. You only have to visit some of the stately homes to appreciate what that means, as around the walls are always large portraits of the ancestors peering from their elevated positions. You can often see a family likeness and every picture tells a story, although the settings and the manner of dress are different.

We are royalty in the kingdom. We too have spiritual ancestors who are cheering us on from the grandstands of heaven (Hebrews 12:1). Each comes from a particular point in history and each has a story to tell.

From generation to generation

God thinks in terms of generations. Many times in the Old Testament, speaking of himself, he said, 'I am the God of Abraham, Isaac and Jacob.' Blessings as well as curses are described as generational (Exodus 20:5-6). Even the life of Jesus was placed in the context of an historical genealogy (Matthew 1:1-17).

The goodness of God was to be proclaimed from father to son, from mother to daughter. David wrote about this in Psalm 145:3-7:

Great is the Lord and most worthy of praise... One generation will commend your works to another... They will speak of the glorious splendour of your majesty, and I will meditate on your wonderful works. They will tell of the power of your awesome works, and I will proclaim your great deeds. They will celebrate your abundant goodness and joyfully sing of your righteousness.

Psalm 71:18 says,
Even when I am old and grey, do not forsake me, O God, till I declare your power to the next generation, your might to all who are to come.

Psalm 78:2-4,
I will utter hidden things, things from of old – what we have heard and known, what our fathers have told us. We will not hide them from our children; we will tell the next generation.

Pass it on

God's goodness, God's power, and God's revelation are to be passed on. Although each generation needs to discover God for themselves, there is also a continuity where the life of God is passed on through generations.

The Old Testament is full of events where God intervened on behalf of his people. He wanted the memory kept alive through succeeding generations by storytelling. This is what they were doing in the covenant renewal ceremonies.

When God sent the plagues upon the Egyptians he told the Israelites to tell their children and grandchildren, *'how I dealt harshly with the Egyptians and how I performed my signs among them…that you may know that I am the Lord'* (Exodus 10:2).

The celebration of the Passover and the consecration of the firstborn son were to be occasions to tell the story again (Exodus 12:26, 13:14). Even today at the Jewish Passover, the youngest child present ritually asks what the ceremony means.

When on the verge of the Promised Land, Moses instructed the Israelites,

Only be careful, and watch yourselves closely so that you do not forget the things your eyes have seen or let them slip from your hearts as long as you live. Teach them to your children and to their children after them. (Deuteronomy 4:9)

The verses I mentioned above from Psalm 78:2-3 say, *'I will utter hidden things, things from of old.'* Hidden things are there to be discovered.

Sometimes they are referred to as 'secret things,' as in Deuteronomy 29:29 which says, *'The secret things belong to the Lord our God, but the things revealed belong to us and to our children for ever, that we may follow all the words of this law.'*

This was said in the context of covenant renewal. It shows that once we have had the revelation of covenant in terms of inheritance, it belongs to us.

We also have a responsibility to pass on not just what has come to us, but those things that have been passed on to us from those who went before. This is 'what our fathers have told us.'

Keys to inheriting the blessings are to 'remember,' and 'value.' Now we turn to the final key, to 'honour.'

Generational turning

The last words of the Old Testament speak of continuity between old and new. I believe that it was the intention of God who orchestrated the books of the Bible, that these verses that speak of generational turning, link the old and new covenants. But more than this, they are crucial to understanding the times in which we live.

The verses in Malachi 4:5-6 explain,

See, I will send you the prophet Elijah before that great and dreadful day of the Lord comes. He will turn the hearts of the father to their children, and the hearts of the children to their fathers, or else I will come and strike the land with a curse.

We read in Luke 1:17 that just as the 'spirit and power' of Elijah rested upon John the Baptist to prepare a way for the coming of the Lord, so that same spirit of Elijah needs to be on us today to prepare a way for the second coming of the Lord. As one song says, *'These are the days of Elijah, declaring the word of the Lord.'*(2) What are the days and what do we need to declare?

One thing to be declared is that hearts need to be turned and honour needs to be restored between the generations. The above verses say that the spirit of Elijah will, 'Turn the hearts of the fathers to their children, and turn the hearts of the children to their fathers.'

This generational healing is desperately needed today with the break-up of family life and the fragmentation of society. But I believe the 'turning' mentioned here is also referring to a spiritual generational turning which is mutual.

A softened heart

And it begins with the heart. It is the hearts that first have to be turned and you cannot turn a hard heart. First of all our hearts need to be turned towards our heavenly Father and intimacy restored.

Pride can have no place here. For spiritual fathers to be willing to give, they need a heart softened by the Holy Spirit. They must be prepared to trust and to entrust what they have received to the next generation.

For their spiritual children to receive, they need an equally soft heart to realize that they still have much to learn from those who have gone before. Personally I am so aware that I have much I can pass on to the next generation, yet I still have much that can be given to me from those of a previous generation and also from the next generation.

John the Baptist stood between the old and new covenants. One could say that he symbolized that turning. Matthew 11:13-14 says, 'All the prophets and the law prophesied until John...he is the Elijah who was to come.'

In that turning is expressed a change of heart from a 'heart of stone' to a 'heart of flesh.' Pointing to the New Covenant, the prophet Ezekiel wrote, 'I will give you a new heart and will put a new spirit within you; I will remove from you your heart of stone and give you a heart of flesh' (Ezekiel 36:26).

Before there can be any generational turning, we need a heart transplant. Our heart of stone needs to be removed and replaced with a heart of flesh, so that we may appreciate our heritage.

They still speak

I have heard so many times in our new churches, 'God is doing a new thing.' I am not cynical about that phrase, but we can be in danger of throwing the baby out with the bathwater. Yes, God does say 'forget the former things; do not dwell on the past' (Isaiah 43:18), but in our arrogance we can act as if all that has gone on before didn't exist and is of no importance.

It is like the scripture where Jesus says we must hate our father and mother. We would all agree that he is speaking in relative terms – that our love for him must be so strong that any other love will be like hate. Forgetting the past does not mean we must ignore it but that in comparison with the 'new things,' it will pale into insignificance. Oh, that the new things we experience captivate us to that extent.

In all of this there's no place for generational arrogance, whether it be about our father's generation, our grandfather's generation, or generations past 'who by faith' still speak, even though they are dead (Hebrews 11:4). Let's be ready to pass on what we have received personally or inherited from previous generations. But as the present generation we must first with softened hearts turn towards those who have gone before and receive what they are giving.

When looking at the beginnings of denominations it is clear that new moves of God are often resisted by those who experienced the previous move of God. In the light of this, we need our hearts to be constantly touched by the Holy Spirit to avoid spiritual arrogance. Elisha got it right as his mentor, Elijah, was taken to heaven, *'Where now is the Lord, the God of Elijah?'* (2 Kings 2:14).

The rod and the sword

The importance of the correct alignment between the generations can be further illustrated with the story found in Exodus 17:10-13. As a young man Joshua was fighting the Amalekites on Moses' orders. As long as Moses held up his hands, the Israelites were winning, but when he got tired and lowered them, the Amalekites were winning. Aaron and Hur understood what was happening and held up his hands until sunset. So we read that Joshua overcame the Amalekite army with the sword.

Moses represents the older or former generation and it was with his rod of authority that he had led the Israelites out of Egypt. The sword was in the hand of Joshua who represents the younger or latter generation. Both were dependent on each other to win the battle before them.

There needed to be an alignment of the generations with the rod and the sword. The success of the sword in the hands of the latter generation is dependent on the rod of authority being correctly positioned in the hand of the former generation. Joshua's success was not solely dependent on the sword in his hands, but on the rod in the hands of Moses.(3)

Honour the fathers and mothers

The only commandment given with a promise is the sixth, *'Honour your father and mother so that you may live long in the land the Lord your God is giving you'* (Exodus 20:12).

You may be an eleventh-hour worker, but those before you have *'borne the burden of the work and the heat of the day'* (Matthew 20:12). They deserve honour. This includes every martyr, every believer who was persecuted and imprisoned, every Christian who was ridiculed for being a forerunner of revelation, everyone who took steps to secure the freedoms we have today.

It also includes those who tenaciously held out for truth, led movements, fought for social justice and carried the gospel to the ends of the earth at great personal cost. Many contended long and hard for breakthrough in areas that we walk in today as a normal part of our Christianity. All of them, like David, served the purposes of God in their generation (Acts 13:36).

We must not allow their quaint ways and cultural mores blur our vision of their value. Even as I write this, I stand in awe of these gems in the rock. It's easy to dishonour others, but honour cuts across the cynical spirit of our age.

God, our source of life

The rebellious followers of Abimelech did not honour Gideon and as a result, the land was cursed. The verses in Malachi that talk about the honouring between generations, comes with a caveat of the covenant curse if there is no honour.

Don't get me wrong. I believe that blessings are more powerful than curses, but turning away from God, our source of life, and disregarding our godly heritage, comes with a consequence. Nevertheless the living water is there, waiting to flood our land again with blessings, like the water in Jacob's well.

The last days

Out of all the Old Testament men and women, Elijah is singled out to be sent again in the last days. The turning of hearts from fathers to their children and from children to their fathers speaks of natural succession through generations, but it also speaks more powerfully of a spiritual succession that we in this generation need to pick up.

Whatever our view may be of the second coming, there is a sense in which every generation needs to behave as if it were the last. We are the generation of Jesus Christ. We need to live prophetically, pointing to the age to come, both by word and deed.

A special prophetic anointing began with Elijah. He was not the first prophet named in the Bible, but it was Elijah who appeared on the Mount of Transfiguration with Moses. They stood one on either side of Christ, representing the law and the prophets of the Old Covenant. Moses, the lawgiver, pointed to the salvation that Jesus was bringing as the fulfilment of the law, and Elijah pointed to the restoration of all things (Matthew 17:1-13).

A prophetic mantle

Elisha was mentored by Elijah and the prophetic mantle fell on him when Elijah was taken to heaven in whirlwind and his cloak, which fell from him, was picked up by Elisha. This cloak symbolized succession to Elijah's anointing and ministry.

Immediately Elisha acted in faith, parting the waters of the River Jordan just as Elijah had done prior to him being taken to heaven. The company of prophets who were watching were left in no doubt that, 'The spirit of Elijah is resting on Elisha' (2 Kings 2:15).

It was the anointing which was transferable, not the spirit of the man Elijah which somehow had lived on. A spiritual lineage had begun. Elisha began to perform many miracles of the same nature as his mentor.

The anointing lives on

There's a strange story we read about in 2 Kings 13:21, where a dead man was thrown into Elisha's tomb. As soon as the body touched Elisha's bones, the man came back to life and stood on his feet. I believe that this tells us prophetically that Elijah's anointing was to live on, and appear in times of preparation for Jesus' first coming and his second coming.

Firstly it would appear in a prophetic individual, John the Baptist. Secondly, it would appear through a prophetic people in the last generation before Christ returns. Both individuals and corporate groups have a message for their generation.

John the Baptist picked up the prophetic anointing for his generation. Luke 1:17 tells us *'He [John] will go on before the Lord in the spirit and power of Elijah, to turn the hearts of the fathers to their children.'* He was *'to make ready a people prepared for the Lord.'*

It's interesting that John describes himself as *'the voice of one calling in the desert'* (John 1:23). His message was to explain to people the days in which they were living. In the Old Testament tradition, he perceived the day of the Lord as a day where there would be a polarization of good and evil, of salvation and judgment (Matthew 3:12). In the light of this, his message was 'Repent! Get ready! Be baptized!'

Elijah will restore all things

But the spiritual line of Elijah did not die when John the Baptist was beheaded. In Matthew 17:11 Jesus said that, *'Elijah comes and will restore all things.'* What does that 'all things' refer to? It is linked to the turning of hearts of the fathers to their children and the turning of the hearts of the children to their fathers.

This speaks of a powerful spiritual generational restoration in the last days. I don't believe it is just referring to immediate generations, but of a turning of hearts back to recapture the anointing of past generations that have been languishing in the grave.

There have been many moves of God that died with no one to carry them forward. Many men and women of God found themselves with no spiritual successor. There are many truths that were restored to the body of Christ in the past that need restoring once again.

We stand in the line of the spirit and power of Elijah. Elisha understood spiritual succession and acted in faith. It's time to metaphorically jump onto the graves of past anointings. We are living in the days when the spirit of the prophet Elijah is about to be released, according to Malachi 4:5-6.

Spiritual impartation

There would have been no Elisha without an Elijah, just as there would be no Joshua without a Moses, and no Timothy without a Paul. In each case there was a transference of the Spirit that enabled them to stand in the line of their mentor.

It was not a natural passing on of knowledge but rather a spiritual impartation that enabled the same anointing to be passed on and become operable. Immediately after Elijah had been taken to heaven, the company of the prophets recognized that, *'the spirit of Elijah is resting on Elisha,'* because of the miracle that he performed.

Standing in the prophetic line

Elijah moved around with what the Bible calls a *'company of the prophets,'* sometimes translated, 'sons of the prophets.' These were not literal sons but indicates to us the relationship that men like Elijah had with the group.

The Lord's prophets were probably their spiritual fathers. Men like Elijah and later Elisha recognized the importance of passing on their anointing. Their hearts were 'turned' to the next generation.

Companies of prophets were to be found at various locations, Bethel, Jericho and Gilgal. The company of prophets from Jericho watched the whole event of Elijah being taken to heaven in a chariot. It appears that as well as verbal instruction, observing and participating in miracles was part of their fathering and mentoring. It was to their credit that these prophets of God looked for successors, someone to stand in the prophetic line.

Gehazi, Elisha's servant, was dismissed when he behaved in an ungodly way, running after personal profit (2 Kings 5:19-27). King Jehoash, who recognised the anointing that resided in Elisha, forfeited it when he was only partially obedient (2 Kings 13:14-20). But the anointing lived on, in Elisha's bones!

The significance of the cloak

The first time we read of Elijah's cloak is when he encounters Elisha ploughing with twelve yoke of oxen. God had told Elijah to anoint him as his successor, which he did by throwing his cloak around him. It's reasonable to assume that they knew each other because Elisha burned his ploughing equipment, breaking with his past life and became Elijah's attendant. The mantle of Elijah was already on Elisha in embryonic form.

I have to smile when I read the story of the taking up of Elijah to heaven. The company of prophets at Bethel asked Elisha if he knew *'the Lord is going to take your master today.'* Elisha's reply was *'Yes, but do not speak of it.'* The same happened with the company of prophets at Jericho. Elijah, too, seemed to know he would be 'taken.' It seems that when these groups got together it was pointless having any sort of conversation, such was their prophetic gifting!

We read of the cloak next when Elijah and Elisha are standing by the Jordan River. We read that *'Elijah took his cloak, rolled it up and struck the water with it. The water divided to the right and to the left, and the two of them crossed over on dry ground'* (2 Kings 2:8).

You can sense the drama of the situation after Elijah is taken to heaven in a whirlwind. As Elijah is caught up, his cloak falls from him and is whisked up by Elisha who then strikes the River Jordan and cries, *'Where now is... the God of Elijah?'* *'When he struck the water, it divided to the right and to the left, and he crossed over'* (2 Kings 2:14).

The same company of prophets that had witnessed Elijah part the water with his cloak now saw Elisha do the same miracle, thus establishing his credentials as his successor in a public way. The cloak symbolized the transference of the mantle of authority and anointing.

Seeing beyond

The prophetic mantle enabled both these men to see beyond the natural to spiritual realities. Although Elijah had been told by God to anoint him as his spiritual successor, he still asked Elisha what he wanted from him before he was taken from him. Elisha's reply was, *'Let me inherit a double portion of your spirit'* (2 Kings 2:9).

It does not mean that Elisha wanted twice as much prophetic anointing as Elijah, but rather to be his successor and continue his work as leader of the prophets. The firstborn son always received a double portion of his father's inheritance (Deuteronomy 21:17). Elijah was a spiritual father to Elisha and the first words Elisha uttered after his parting was, 'My father! My father!' (2 Kings 2:12).

Elijah gave an intriguing reply to Elisha's request which left the answer squarely in the hands of God. He said, 'If you see me when I am taken from you, it will be yours – otherwise not.' He knew that anointing came from vision (2 Kings 2:10).

What a tremendous exit from this world! Elijah certainly saw beyond the natural. While the astonished prophetic onlookers only witnessed the disappearance of their beloved old prophet, Elisha was a player in a scene that could be straight from a Hollywood movie.

As the two were walking along together, a chariot of fire pulled by horses of fire swept between them, and Elijah was taken to heaven in the whirlwind. Elisha saw and recognized that the true power behind Israel lay not in earthly kings and armies, but in angelic protection.

This vision stayed with him. Later in his ministry, when surrounded by the horses and chariots of a natural army, he drew his strength from the certainty of the spiritual army of horses and chariots of fire which surrounded him (2 Kings 6:13-17).

So it was not only moving in the miraculous, but 'seeing beyond' that established Elisha in the prophetic line of succession.

Spiritual succession

Moses was a man who was mindful of the next generation. He fathered Joshua who had been his assistant since a young man (Numbers 11:28) and publicly confirmed him as his successor to take the Israelites into Canaan (Numbers 31:7-8).

As well as a great leader and the law-giver to Israel, Moses was a prophet. The Bible record states that it was by a prophet that the Israelites were led out of Egypt (Hosea 12:13).

There is a story in the book of Numbers that illustrates not just the transference of anointing, but captures the heart of the man who wants to see this prophetic anointing be on all God's people. Under a prophetic anointing, Moses spoke words, very likely without realizing all the implications of their fulfilment in successive generations.

Moses made 70 of the elders of Israel stand around the tent of meeting. God took the Spirit that was on Moses and put it on the elders, and when this happened they prophesied as a sign of the anointing. Two other elders who had not gone to the tent also had the Spirit come to rest on them. Moses' response was, *'I wish that all the Lord's people were prophets and that the Lord would put his Spirit on them'* (Numbers 11:29).

It's as if Moses looked down through history with the eyes of faith and 'saw beyond.' The hope he expressed that all God's people would be prophets was fulfilled with the outpouring of the Holy Spirit on the day of Pentecost, a day when the Spirit of God fell on 120 men and women in the upper room in Jerusalem.

Continuing unhindered

Peter gave a prophetic explanation of what was happening, quoting from Joel 2:28-29, when he said,

In the last days, God says, I will pour my Spirit on all people. Your sons and daughters will prophesy, your young men will see visions, your old men will dream dreams. Even on my servants, both men and women, I will pour out my Spirit in those days, and they will prophesy. (Acts 2:17-18)

Then in his speech to the people of Israel, Peter explains that this is not just a one-off event: *'The promise [of the Holy Spirit] is for you and your children, and for all who are far off'* (Acts 2:39).

The Holy Spirit line was established and sealed with prophetic manifestation. God meant it to continue unhindered through history until the time when prophesies will cease and tongues will be stilled (1 Corinthians 13:8).

Honour for what they did

In honouring others, we put ourselves in the position to receive mantles. We all have feet of clay, even revivalists who shook nations. It's easy to find flaws in anyone's character and criticise them for not finishing well. But it's important to honour them for what they did rather than what they didn't do.

The following true story illustrates this point. It happened to the same Louise who saw the angel I wrote about in the last chapter.

I was lying on the floor in worship in school(4) and I felt intensity in the air. I told God I was ready because I knew something was going to happen. So I said 'I am ready' three times and on the third time I realized I couldn't hear anything any more. I opened my eyes and I was standing there in Moriah Chapel and Evan Roberts was preaching.

The chapel was packed out, he walked down from the pulpit and stood in front of me but before I could say anything to him he said to me, 'Redeem me.' He paused and it was as if he was saying, 'I know how history is going to see me.' I started telling him that it's not how I see him, and he said, 'I know how history is going to see me.' He looked at all the people in the chapel and smiled, 'But I would have done anything for this, anything to see our country ablaze.'

At this point I was on my knees crying and he got down to my level and said, 'What would you do to see Wales ablaze again?' and then I closed my eyes and when I opened them I was back in twin view.

For what seemed like hours afterwards I was sitting in school and I could see them talking on stage but I couldn't hear anything they were saying; all I could hear was him preaching. I was not fully back in my body for a good while. I am kind of blown away by this. It blew my mind!

Receive what they carried

Much has been written on why the Welsh revival only lasted around 18 months, and criticism has been levied against Evan Roberts. It's not the place of this book to look at that. I would say, yes, we can always learn from history, but we should honour the heart and spirit of the man.

It is men and women like Evan Roberts and their hunger after God that brought heaven down. In doing that we can receive from them what they carried in varying degrees. Some will catch their passion, and a few will pick up a mantle that has been laid in the grave, waiting for someone to run with it again.

Our heritage is our inheritance

Some in our generation lament like Jeremiah, *'Our inheritance has been turned over to aliens, our homes to foreigners. We have become orphans and fatherless, our mothers like widows'* (Lamentations 5:2-3). It can seem as if our birthright has been stolen, but I hope that by now you will see that you have deep roots and a more-than-rich spiritual heritage.

Our heritage can become our inheritance when we stand like Ezekiel in the valley of dry bones and prophesy, *'Dry bones, hear the word of the Lord'* (Ezekiel 37:4). God has got something to say to you about the past, your past, and there will be a clicking into place.

We are connected!

Ask the former generations and find out what their fathers learned, for we were born only yesterday and know nothing and our days on earth are but a shadow. Will they not instruct you and tell you? Will they not bring forth words from their understanding?
Job 8:8-10

Endnotes

1. A. Skevington Wood, *The Burning Heart*, Cliff College Publishing, Sheffield, 2001, p 19.

2. Robin Mark, *Days of Elijah*, 1996.

3. This revelation was from a talk by Banning Leibsher, Jesus Culture, Bethel Church, Redding, California, USA, Slough, UK, 2006.

4. Bethel School of Supernatural Ministry, Bethel Church, Redding, California, USA.

11
Sons and Daughters of Laughter

Gather the people together, and I will give them water. Then Israel sang this song: 'Spring up, O well! Sing about it, about the well that the princes dug, that the nobles of the people sank – the nobles with sceptres and staffs.' Numbers 21:16-17

The last piece of the puzzle

We're now nearing the end of our journey, but there's one more piece of the puzzle to complete the picture. It began with a prophetic word given me by the same person who first told me back in 1996 that revival was in my blood and I'd better do some digging! These are the exact words that were spoken to me in 2009:

Genesis 26:18: Isaac reopened the wells that had been stoned up in the time of the Philistines, stoned up after Abraham, the man of faith had died. And I want to tell you, you have an authority to open wells – and it's the son of laughter, the daughter of laughter – Isaac, laughter, reopened the wells.

It will be the counter of the religious stones and stones of fear that have stopped up the wells. Ancient wells of revival will be opened. God has given you in your hands to literally dig open these wells with others on the place of repentance for religion and fear. And you will reopen the wells that have been stopped up by the Philistines. And these are ancient wells where there is fresh water.

Heir to the blessings

So what's the story behind this? Wells were crucial to life in the ancient Near East. They were the source of life without which these desert nomads couldn't exist.

Water is still an issue in the land of Israel today. I remember when I was there in 1998, our Israeli guide was talking to us about the Arab-Israeli War of 1967. During that war there was a struggle to capture the Golan Heights in the north of the country, which were an important source of water.

The guide said that whoever controlled these mountains controlled Israel, since it was at the source that the springs of water could be stopped. Then he said this little phrase that lodged in my mind, 'He who has the water has the land.'

Abraham's son, Isaac, was the heir to the covenant of blessing given to Abraham, and this included the land and the wells that Abraham had dug. Isaac walked into his inheritance, he didn't work for it. He inherited the blessings. He became very wealthy and received a hundred-fold increase on the crops he had planted (Genesis 26:12). The source of his natural wealth was in the wells that his father had dug. Isaac knew he had the water rights!

Isaac staked his claim

At that time he was living in Gerar, the land of the Philistines, whose king was Abimelech. Like his father he had found favour with the king, but some of the Philistines were jealous of his wealth. Already in his life the promises of God were being fulfilled; God was blessing him.

Recognizing the importance of the wells, the Philistines filled them with earth. This was a tactic of war. What did Isaac do? He re-opened the wells that had been dug in the time of his father Abraham and he gave them the same names as his father had done (Genesis 26:18).

Isaac recognized the source of his blessing. He knew that he must remove the rubble that the Philistines had put in the wells to stop the flow of water. His servants dug open the wells and also dug new ones (Genesis 26:19-21) and Isaac was able to say, *'Now the Lord has given us room and we will flourish in the land'* (Genesis 26:22).

That night God appeared to him and reassured Isaac that he was with him, that all the blessings of the covenant belonged to him and his descendants. In response Isaac built an altar, pitched his tent and dug another well. This was a personal prophetic act, staking a claim to his inheritance.

Lessons from a well opener

Isaac knew who his father was and he knew who he was. He understood the covenant, he knew his heritage and his rights of inheritance. His was no poverty mentality. He knew that his father's wells had made him wealthy. All he did was find the wells, unblock them and then the blessings of water were his. He honoured his father Abraham by giving them the same names as he had.

I hope the parallel is obvious, but I'll spell it out. Because our fathers in the faith dug deep wells, we are spiritually wealthy. Like Isaac, the 'water rights' are ours!

But it didn't end there, as Isaac dug more wells in the land of his inheritance. For us, too, there's no limit to fresh springs of water for us to discover.

Quenching the Spirit

The prophecy said that it was the religious stones and stones of fear that have stopped up the wells. In the biblical narrative it was the Philistines, a tribe who were constantly at war with and harassing the Israelites, who were filling the wells with earth to stop the flow. How true it has been that religion has come as a formidable quencher of vital Christianity.

I've given many examples in this book where man has sought to control a move of God with rules and regulations. When a religious spirit dominates, it prevents the Holy Spirit from leading and maintaining the vital flow of life. Time and again, charismatic life has been replaced by institutionalism. As well as stones of control, stones of fear have been lobbed in wells dug by our forefathers by those afraid that the status quo is being disturbed; afraid, too, that their man-made structures will come toppling down, bringing with them their ecclesiastical positions. All this has more to do with shoring up egos, rather than advancing the kingdom.

Why do revivals cease? Why do moves of God wane? Often you don't have to look far.

Disputes at the wells

When Isaac started to open up the old wells and then dig new ones in land that rightfully belonged to him, there was conflict between his herdsmen and the herdsman of Gerar about the water rights. This is another picture of disputes that can occur when there are fresh moves of the Holy Spirit. The new thing that the Holy Spirit is doing often comes into conflict with a past move. There is a propensity for control and suspicion if the Holy Spirit does not move in ways that we think fitting or are comfortable with.

Isaac was a man of peace. When Abimelech, king of the Philistines came to see him, he acknowledged that Isaac was living under the blessing and favour of God and that they would leave him alone. As it says in Proverbs 16:7, *'When a man's ways are pleasing to the Lord, he makes even his enemies to live at peace with him.'*

All of grace

Isaac just walked into his inheritance; his was the land and the wells were there. It was all because of the covenant. He didn't have to work or strive to obtain it, because it was rightfully his, it was all of grace.

Religion is works-based, striving to achieve a self-imposed goal, and rewards are dependent on what we do. Conversely, Spirit-led Christianity is born from rest, lived out in rest and enjoying the eternal Sabbath with God.

So what can we do about religion and fear? Repentance means to change the way you think and live differently. Striving, control and fear are counter to the life that God intends us to live, a life characterised by rest, freedom and love.

There is no fear in love and if we know that we are loved and accepted by God, there is no need to strive and control. Simply living and acting in grace is coming in the opposite spirit. We are then countering the religious stones that block the wells.

Joy made flesh

Back to the prophecy: 'and it's the son of laughter, the daughter of laughter – Isaac, laughter, reopened the wells.'

The name Isaac means, 'He laughs.' Laughter surrounded his birth. Abraham was a hundred and Sarah was ninety, far too old to have children. Yet God had told them they would be a father and mother of nations!

Abraham's response was to fall face down and laugh (Genesis 17:17). Sarah laughed too (Genesis 18:12-15). When Isaac was born Sarah said, *'God has brought me laughter, and everyone who hears about this will laugh with me'* (Genesis 21:6).

It was Isaac, laughter, who reopened the wells.

We are descendants of Abraham by faith and inheritors of blessings (Galatians 3:9). In that line we stand as sons and daughters of Isaac, sons and daughters of laughter and laughter will open the wells.

Laughter is what children do when they are playing. It is an explosion of joy, it's cathartic. It stops us taking ourselves too seriously. It is the exact opposite of striving, fear and control. It's religion that doesn't allow laughter. Spirit-filled Christians should be able to laugh, to play, to have fun, and yes to dance which I've heard described as 'joy made flesh'!(1)

A different approach

Some of the thoughts in this book, especially in these last three chapters, have made an impact in my spirit before I was quite able to explain them with my mind. There's been a gradual unfolding of understanding, with a movement from heart to head.

After all, how can laughter unblock wells? Does this mean that we go and stand in a physical location, an identified 'Shechem' or 'well' and laugh? Maybe so, if the Spirit leads you, but there is more to it that that!

Laughter represents a whole new way of looking at things. It's a playful response to life itself.

We can all understand the idea of knowing and remembering our history, valuing our inheritance and honouring our fathers and nod our heads in agreement. Laughter, on the other hand, is different. Yet all of these are qualitative rather than quantative concepts and can't be measured. They are attitudes and approaches rather than formulas.

It's a mistake to think that there are spiritual formulas we can follow to unblock wells or pick up mantles. We can't just know our history, find the well, identify what blocked it, repent and hey presto it's open again, or find a person in our history we resonate with, learn about him or her and what they did, and by faith claim their anointing. It's not just $a + b = c$.

For sure, understanding Britain's history with God is a starting point. I trust the chapters in this book have given you a greater appreciation of our spiritual past and the men and women who co-operated with the Holy Spirit in shaping it. We need to be Spirit-led like them, and not formula driven.

The delight of serendipity

For the past 300 years, Newtonian physics dominated our thinking in the west with its mechanistic worldview of cause and effect. But now quantum physics has opened up a whole new reality to us. It is said, 'we can learn from new science to be more playful, to develop a different relationship with discovery.'(2)

One scientist said that now if you hear laughter in the laboratory, you can tell that things are going well and that something worth looking at has started to happen.(3) Predictability has given way to the delight of serendipity.

The earth is not simply the stage on which the drama of life is performed. No, the world seems to be built up in accordance with the structure and dynamics of play. In contrast to Newton's one-sided orderly mechanical picture of the world, modern physics and biology stress the idea of indeterminacy.

This is not a matter of blind chance, since there are fundamental limitations like the limits of species and of time and space. These represent as it were the rule of the cosmic game in which the elements of indeterminacy represent the creative possibility of something new, of a surprising shift (as in a mutation).(4)

It's always fresh

So in looking to unblock the wells, reclaim our spiritual inheritances and take on mantles we need the understanding that we are inheriting the life, not the methods or structures. The prophecy said that these will be 'ancient wells where there is fresh water.' When Isaac's servants dug to find more springs in the land of his inheritance, there was great excitement as they shouted, 'We've found water!' (Genesis 26:32).

As well as the joy of the fresh flow from the previously blocked ancient wells, the new discoveries will be like the laughter in the laboratory! However we access the water, it's always fresh because in God we always live in the now.

Spring up, O well!

In their wilderness wanderings, water was a constant problem for the Israelites. On one occasion they reached a place called Beer, a common name in the desert meaning 'a well.' God told Moses to gather the people together and sing 'the song of the well' and he would give them water (Numbers 21:16-17).

So that's what they did. They sang, 'Spring up, O well! Sing about it – about the well that the princes dug, that the nobles of the people sank – the nobles with sceptres and staffs.'

It was a popular song and frequently sung when a well or spring was found. There were several customs surrounding this, but they all involved dancing and singing songs to the well or even holding a feast to induce a steady flow of water! It was a time of celebration, fun and laughter.

One custom involved the enactment of a pantomime. Wherever a well was found it was lightly covered over and then the desert clan leader would 'open' it again as they sang. In the re-enactment of digging it and reopening it, they then regarded it as their property.(5) Isaiah 12:3 encourages us to draw water from the wells of salvation with joy.

Celebrating covenant

As well as remembering, honouring and valuing the work of the 'princes and nobles,' the people were actually celebrating the covenant and releasing the blessings of the water.

For us, the 'princes and nobles' are our forefathers who dug the wells in our history. So let's celebrate, dance, have fun, play, laugh, sing as we say, 'Thank you, Jesus' for what he has done. Let's release faith that the blessings contained are for a thousand generations as we declare, 'Spring up, O well!'

This is our celebration of covenant as we remember, honour and value Britain's history with God. He says, 'I am your God' and we respond, 'We are your people' (Jeremiah 31:33).

As we do this we are joining in 'The perfect covenant [which is like] like a mutual dance of Father, Son and Holy Spirit spilling over into creation.'(6) It's a dance of romance and intimacy and that's why the marriage metaphor is so apt.

A wedding

Zippporah was the bride that understood covenant. The prophecy I was given which said that 'covenant is the key to opening up the wells in the UK' also said that God wants to raise up Zipporahs as a bride to uphold the covenant (Chapter 9). We, the church, are that bride. Remember Matt's song, 'Awaken Britain' in the introduction to this book: he sings about the bride being drawn back to her lover in a covenant relationship.

Awaken Britain

You're calling your beloved back to you
In these times we awaken to your truth
We're drawing near to you
We're drawing near to you
You're calling your Bride back to you
To be pure and holy

We're drawing near to you
We're drawing near to you

Chorus

These wells of my heart are overflowing
These wells of my heart are overflowing
And your love, your love is never failing
And your love, your love is never failing

Your love unfailing, grace abounding
I surrender all to you

There will be a future celebration when the covenant between God and his people will be consummated. The Bible calls it *'the wedding supper of the Lamb'* (Revelation 19:9). In the meantime we can celebrate that future grace, *'a feast of rich food for all peoples, a banquet of aged wine – the best of meats and the finest of wines.'* (Isaiah 25:6) as the bride who understands the covenantal blessings that are ours.

Royalty at play

The Bible is full of metaphors. As well as being the bride of Christ, we are sons and daughters of the King. We are royalty!

In Britain we are familiar with the idea of the monarchy. As I said in the introduction, I live in Windsor, so am constantly reminded of our heritage. This town, called the 'Royal Borough,' has been overshadowed by Windsor Castle for over a thousand years.

Royals know who they are and live from that position of privilege. Unlike some of the kings and queens of past centuries, today they enjoy security in the institution they belong to.

The royalty are royal even in times of leisure! As sons and daughters of the King, we can also be sons and daughters of laughter. Secure in who we are, we can be free to laugh and play.

Stewardship of history

As I've said in previous chapters, royalty is built on generational succession with a deep understanding of history. Part of the dilemma facing royalty today is the delicate balancing act of being a modern monarchy whilst appreciating and stewarding the past.

I believe the stewardship of Britain's history with God, his-story, is in our hands. There's a telling story in Psalm 78 where we read about men from the tribe of Ephraim who *'turned back on the day of battle'* even though they were armed with bows. In battle they couldn't bring themselves to face the enemy and the reasons given was a lack of appreciation of God's covenant and forgetting the wonders and miracles he had done for their forefathers (Psalm 78:9-12).

Earlier on in that Psalm we read,

I will utter hidden things, things from of old – what we have heard and known, what our fathers have told us. We will not hide them from our children; we will tell the next generation the praiseworthy deeds of the Lord, his power, and the wonders he has done...he commanded our forefathers to teach their children, so that the next generation would know them, even the children yet to be born, and they in turn would tell their children. Then they would put their trust in God and would not forget his deeds. (Psalm 78:2-7)

How we need to value the record and keep the stories alive.

A new community

To end with, a story still in the making which brings together many of the strands in this book illustrating what 'redigging the wells' can look like in an actual 21st century context. In 1989 one 'new church' in Southampton, on the south coast of England, bought and renovated an old Wesleyan Methodist Central Hall which stands in the heart of the city. It's New Community Church led by Pioneer leaders, Billy and Caroline Kennedy. (7)

Between 1886 and 1945, Methodist Central Halls were being built in many towns and cities in this country. As their name suggests they were all in central locations, looking more like imposing civic buildings than traditional churches. This one in Southampton was built in 1925 to seat 800 people.

Sometime into New Community occupying the building they discovered documents relating to the original purpose of this particular Central Hall. It was evident that it was not just used for religious services but was a hub for philanthropic and charitable organisations. These Methodists of eight or so decades ago were active in their community in social care and education. At the hall they provided entertainment, showing religious and educational films, and making it a place to meet with friends. These all helped to attract weekly congregations from the nearby working-class housing. It had also been a place where George Jeffries, in 1927, held revival meetings and in 1947, Billy Graham preached his first sermon on English soil.

Celebrating together
The Kennedys realised they were fulfilling the original mandate as they sought to build a relational church which reached out into the community in the same way. They are now working in partnership with the Southampton Methodist Circuit to bring other old buildings back to use for the benefit the city.

As 'sons and daughters of laughter,' New Community Church are committed to celebrating the goodness of God, having fun together and being the example of 'joy made flesh.' They are expressing non-religious Christianity. As they do, the wells are being unblocked.

A shared heritage
But it doesn't end there. Many in the new churches look back to the days of the Wesleys as part of their heritage. In the light of this it is interesting that discussions are underway between more than one New Church Network and the Methodist Church in the UK. Recognising this shared heritage, they are exploring what this might mean for mission in 21st century Britain looking at similar partnerships with Methodist districts across the country. Old and new are coming together in a fresh and exciting way.

History and prophecy join hands
Now that you have read about some of Britain's history with God, my prayer is that you have been captured by the spiritual inheritance that

is ours. I hope this has started you on your own journey of discovery, because there is so much more that I have not been able to write about in one short book.

Every story featured has originated in the heart of God. As he found men and women ready to partner with him, together they brought heaven down to earth.

It could be easy to fall into a lament with the 'if only' striving mode of prayer for God to move in certain ways again. Remembering, honouring and valuing are our attitude of approach, while secure in our royal identity. From a place of rest and celebration, we decree as sons and daughters of laughter 'Spring up, O well!' and 'Dry bones, hear the word of the Lord!'

We live in exciting days. This book has been all about how understanding our history can help shape today's reality. I believe we live in the days that *'many prophets and kings wanted to see'* (Luke 10:24). A move of God can begin with us as we unblock the ancient water sources and at the same time plunge into fresh wells we dig in the land of our inheritance. In doing so, history and prophecy join hands.

All the springs of the great deep burst forth and the floodgates of the heavens were opened. And rain fell on the earth.
(Genesis 7:11-12)

Endnotes

1. Jean-Jacques Suurmond, *Word and Spirit at Play*, SCM Press, London, UK, 1994, p 94.

2. Margaret J. Wheatley, *Leadership and the New Science*, Berrett-Koehler Publishers, San Francisco, 1999, p 161.

3. Ibid., p 162.

4. Suurmond, op.cit., p 40.

5. www.jewishencyclopedia.com

6. Suurmond, op.cit., p 9.

7. Pioneer is a network of more than 80 churches in the UK (at the time of writing) that emerged from the Charismatic Renewal in the early 1980s.